PLOT

ABOUT THE AUTHOR

Ansen Dibell is the pen name of a teacher/writer/editor whose five-novel science fiction series, *The Rule of One*, has been internationally published. After earning MA, MFA, and Ph.D. degrees from the Writers' Workshop of the University of Iowa, Dibell went on to a diversity of jobs including delivering phone books door to door and serving as a college president.

Active with community writers' groups and college level writing programs, Dibell calls herself a *writing coach:* "Many people contend that creativity can't be taught. Maybe not. But, like any other sophisticated performance skill—from playing the violin to Bowling for Dollars—it certainly *can* be coached."

When not busy coaching, Dibell is a freelance writer and editor in Cincinnati.

PLOT

BY

ANSEN DIBELL

WRITER'S DIGEST BOOKS

CINCINNATI, OHIO

Plot. Copyright © 1988 by Ansen Dibell. Printed and bound in the United States of America. All rights reserved. No part of this book may be reproduced in any form or by any electronic or mechanical means including information storage and retrieval systems without permission in writing from the publisher, except by a reviewer, who may quote brief passages in a review. Published by Writer's Digest Books, an imprint of F+W Publications, Inc., 4700 East Galbraith Road, Cincinnati, Ohio 45236; (800)289-0963. First paperback edition 1999.

Other fine Writer's Digest Books are available from your local bookstore or direct from the publisher.

Visit our Web site at www.writersdigest.com for information on more resources for writers.

To receive a free weekly e-mail newsletter delivering tips and updates about writing and about Writer's Digest products, send an e-mail with the message "Subscribe Newsletter" to newsletter-request@writersdigest.com or register directly at our Web site at www.writersdigest.com.

11 10 09 08 07   11 10 9 8 7

Library of Congress has catalogued hard copy edition as follows:

Dibell, Ansen
    Plot/Ansen Dibell.
    p. cm.
    Includes index.
    ISBN-13: 978-0-89879-303-3 (hardcover)
    ISBN-10: 0-89879-303-3 (hardcover)
    ISBN-13: 978-0-89879-946-0 (pbk: alk. paper)
    ISBN-10: 0-89879-946-5 (pbk: alk. paper)
    1. Fiction—Technique.   2. Plots (Drama, novel, etc.)
I. Title.
PN3378.D5   1988   87-26587
808.3—dc19   CIP

fw
F+W PUBLICATIONS, INC.

Design by Christine Aulicino

CONTENTS

COMING TO PLOT THE HARD WAY

If you're like me and most of the writers I've known over the years in writers' groups, at conferences and in classes, you're coming to plot the hard way. A scene, a bit of dialogue, a character sets you happily scribbling or keyboarding away. And then, too often, something happens. The story starts to slow and go sour, dead ending in frustrated scraps of revision. It's eventually tossed with the rest of the might-have-beens—in the bottom of your sock drawer or even in the wastebasket.

Or maybe you want to write a story based on real life and real incidents. That should be a cinch, right? All the events really happened; the characters are people you know. Nothing easier than writing it all down, you think confidently. Just change the names and locale, and you're set.

But then the events, so compelling when they happened and when you thought about them, bog down in detail and explanations. The familiar people you felt certain would be enthralling characters turn into jabbering trolls.

You feel the silent inner thud that tells you that truth—or, more accurately, fact-based fiction—is no more a guarantee against writing dull, unconvincing tales than is inventing the whole thing from the start.

Begin to sound familiar yet?

Have you ever had what seemed like a vivid story idea that fizzled out as soon as you got your first words on paper? Or have you written a story you thought was great and had it come back with a rejection slip commenting that it "seemed distant and uninvolving"? What's *distant,* for heaven's sake? What do you do now?

Or you're starting your second novel while the first one is in the mail, and somewhere about page 90 you find one of your subplots is becoming a lot more interesting than your main plot. It seems to want to take over the whole book. You get bored whenever you have to return to the main character's problems, which now seem to you about as dramatic as watching ice cream melt.

Or you've written and sold some fiction by good gut instinct. And now the problem arises: how did you do it before? And how can you do it again? You want to bring your unconscious craft under greater conscious control, so that you can make choices, not just blunder through until something goes wrong, or right.

Are you one of the writers whose instincts are better than their knowledge, who write merrily along when inspiration strikes and bog down in despair when inspiration inevitably fails?

If this list of woes sounds at all familiar, you're in good company.

Melville wrote a large chunk of *Moby Dick* thinking that the pivotal figure was going to be a man named (I'm not kidding) Bulkington. Read the first couple of chapters and notice all the build-up about Bulkington, who's then abruptly washed overboard the first day the *Pequod* leaves harbor and is never heard of again. What happened? Melville had discovered a character named Ahab. Melville wasn't a tidy writer: the original beginning is still there. Alas, poor Bulkington.

Similarly, J. R. R. Tolkien has confessed that about a third of the way through *The Fellowship of the Ring*, some ruffian named Strider confronted the hobbits in an inn, and Tolkien was in despair. He didn't know who Strider was, where the book was going, or what to write next. Strider turns out to be no lesser person than Aragorn, the unrecognized and uncrowned king of all the forces of good, whose restoration to rule is, along with the destruction of the evil ring, the engine that moves the plot of the whole massive trilogy, *The Lord of the Rings*.

Neither Melville nor Tolkien knew what he was getting into,

going in. And neither was, at that point, a beginner.

It happens, one time or another, to everybody. Fiction is so nearly like life that a good fiction nearly always changes under your hands, takes on an atmosphere, a feel, a will of its own. Your subconscious is sending you smoke signals: ideas seem to come out of nowhere and flash onto the page. Sometimes, as with Ahab and Strider, that's for the good, and a wise, experienced writer recognizes that what was imagined along the way is stronger than what was originally intended. But sometimes, the turning of the material into its own shape can be destructive, and the story collapses into mismatched fragments.

The subconscious sends up, not only smoke signals, but smoke screens that can obscure, distort, and sometimes destroy your vision of what you're trying to create.

You can make outlines and try to lock out that kind of change. But you know, and I know, that writing is as much a process of discovery as it is one of invention, and the more serious you are about your writing and the more complex the story you're trying to tell, the more likely it is to start creating itself in unexpected ways.

Unfortunately, the inevitable flip side is that the story is also much more likely to take a quick dive into the sock drawer, unless you can identify what's going wrong and choose an effective strategy for coping with it.

There are really two problems, then: creating plot, and controlling plot. In your first tries at fiction, whether short stories or novels, you're apt to be coping more with the creating part of the problem. The more experienced you are, the more apt you are to be dealing with the difficulties of controlling plot—which sometimes involves simply getting out of the plot's way and discovering your Strider, your Ahab, your own special story.

Whatever stage you're at now, it's important to recognize that all the false starts, the fizzled conclusions, the saggy, random middles, the corners you paint your characters into, and all the rest of the trolls that pop up from under what seemed safe bridges are a normal part of fiction writing. One of the writers' corollaries to Murphy's Law should read: *Every Plot Starts to Go Wrong Just After the First Big Scene.* The exceptions to this rule, in a writing life, you could fold into an average-size paper airplane.

Expect it, accept it. Any story worth writing is going to bring problems, for you as well as for your characters. As in fiction, the interesting part will be how those problems get solved.

Meeting a problem only means you're smart enough to know one when you see one: it's not a short-cut to the sock drawer. Don't give up. When initial inspiration and enthusiasm sag, that's when craft and experience can get you rolling again. Whatever doesn't kill your story dead in its tracks is likely to make it, and you, stronger.

There's life after the sock drawer—and maybe life *in* it for stories you gave up on too soon. There are ways to create, fix, steer, and discover plots—ways which, over a writing life, you'd eventually puzzle out for yourself. They aren't laws. They're an array of choices, things to try, once you've put a name to the particular problem your story is facing *now*.

That's what this book is about: learning to put a name to the problem and then deciding which, of the whole array of possible choices, is the one that's appropriate for *your* story, whether short fiction or long.

Whether you're writing fact-based fiction or spinning the whole thing out of your head, you have the responsibility of creating a satisfying, self-consistent, independent world and making it all come alive on the page.

Other writers have evolved methods of making worlds out of words. You can use them too.

CHAPTER 1

WHAT IS PLOT?

THE COMMON DEFINITION OF PLOT is that it's whatever happens in a story. That's useful when talking about completed stories, but when we're considering stories being written, it's about as useful as saying that a birthday cake is a large baked confection with frosting and candles. It doesn't tell you how to make one.

Plot is built of significant events in a given story—significant because they have important consequences. Taking a shower isn't necessarily plot, or braiding one's hair, or opening a door. Let's call them incidents. They happen, but they don't lead to anything much. No important consequences.

But if the character is Rapunzel, and the hair is what's going to let the prince climb to her window, braiding her hair is a crucial action. If the character is Bluebeard's newest wife, opening the forbidden door which reveals the corpses of her predecessors is a pivotal point. Taking a shower is, in *Psycho*, considerably more dramatic and shocking than the theft of a large sum of money, both in itself and in terms of its later repercussions. By the way they're weighted and presented, by what they lead to, these events are transformed from incident to plot.

A grammar school play in which a little girl dresses up in a frame of chickenwire and canvas to portray a ham, representing Pork, could be trivial, a mere incident; but in Harper Lee's *To Kill a Mockingbird*, the chickenwire costume is what prevents Scout Finch from being stabbed by a man with a murderous grudge against her lawyer father.

The wearing of the costume has important consequences and makes a meaningful difference in the story's fictional world.

It's a cause that has significant effects. Cause and effect: that's what makes plot.

The Border of Actuality

Plot is the things characters do, feel, think, or say, that make a difference to what comes afterward.

If you once thought about dying your hair pink but never acted on the thought, that tells something about your psychology, but it's not a potential story plot. If you really went ahead and *did* it, that not only tells about your psychology but creates repercussions, like a stone tossed in a pond. *That* might become the basis for a story like Fitzgerald's "Bernice Bobs Her Hair."

Thought or emotion crosses the line into plot when it becomes action and causes reactions. Until then, attitudes, however interesting in themselves, are just potential, just cloudy possibilities. They're static. They're not going anywhere. Nothing comes of them.

No thought, in and of itself, is plot. No action, however dramatic, is plot if the story would have been about the same if it hadn't happened at all. Any action, however seemingly trivial, can be vital and memorable if it has significant consequences and changes the story's outcome.

Plotting is a way of looking at things. It's a way of deciding what's important and then *showing* it to be important through the way you construct and connect the major events of your story. It's the way you show things mattering.

What's at Stake?

For a reader to care about your story, there has to be something at stake—something of value to gain, something of value to be lost. Paul Boles, in his book *Storycrafting*, called it "wrestling," and I like that image because, unlike "theme" or "message," it doesn't imply something that could be painted on a billboard or winkled out of a fortune cookie. Wrestling is something specific happening: two strong forces are meeting, one of them triumphing over the other—for better or for worse.

One of the forces may be external to the main character (protagonist): a villain, an opponent, a set of circumstances, a feature of the environment or of the landscape. Or both forces may be within the protagonist: the fear of doing something wrestling with the need to do it; a sense of injury wrestling with love or admiration, as with a person of any age trying to come to terms with a demanding parent.

Bringing out the importance of seemingly small things leads to subtlety, drama; showing large things grappling and clashing is melodrama, of which more in Chapter 7.

You have to convince the reader not only that something is happening, but that what's happening matters intensely—not just to the writer, but to the characters involved.

In Golding's *Lord of the Flies*, what's at stake is survival itself. A group of boys are trying to stay alive, solely by their own efforts, on an otherwise uninhabited tropical island. At least, that's the external form of their struggle. Internally, it's the battle between fear and courage, distrust of the unknown and the will to find out, as played out within individual characters like the protagonist, Ralph; visionary Simon; and Jack, leader of the hunters. It's not only survival at stake, but a particular, civilized kind of survival.

In other words, there can be an outer plot and an inner one which in some sense mirrors and reinforces it, or conflicts and contrasts with it. Or either outer plot or inner plot may stand alone as the main focus of the necessary struggle played out in actions, through scenes.

MAKING A SCENE

If you've been to a writer's conference or a creative writing class, or if you've read any books on fiction writing, you've already heard the major principle that older writers are always telling younger writers: SHOW, DON'T TELL. As I hope I've *shown* (and maybe told, a little: but this isn't fiction), it's an important concept that's *very* risky not to take very seriously indeed.

Showing, in fiction, means creating scenes. You have to be able to cast your ideas in terms of something happening, people talking and doing, an event going on while the reader reads. If you're not writing scenes, you may be writing fine essays, or speeches, or sermons—but you're not writing fiction.

A definition: A *scene* is one connected and sequential action, together with its embedded description and background material. It seems to happen just as if a reader were watching and listening to it happen. It's built on talk and action. It's dramatized, *shown*, rather than being summarized or talked about. In some ways, it's like a little independent story; some short stories, in fact, are all one single scene.

A scene isn't a random stretch of action. It arises for a reason, and it's going somewhere. It has meaning. It has a point: at least one thing that needs to be shown or established at that spot in a story. That can be something as basic as the fact that your main character wants, this once, to walk his dog in peace without being pestered by an amorous neighbor or something as subtle as your main character's realization that the tolerance she has prided herself on is really just a mask for indifference. Attitudes turning into motives, meeting resistance, creating conflict, and leading to consequences—becoming plot.

A scene can convey many things: moods, attitudes, a sense of place and time, an anticipation of what's to come, a reflection of what's past. But first and foremost, a scene must advance the plot and demonstrate the characters. You may not fully know what a given scene's job is, whether simple or complex, until you've written it. You may need to go back then and cut away the things that would mislead a reader, and add things to support, lead into, and highlight that scene's special chores in the context of the whole story. But when the story is finished, no matter how many rewrites it takes, you ought to be able to name to yourself what each scene brought out, how it developed the characters, how it showed action or led toward consequences.

Scenes can be long or short—just a paragraph, or a dozen

pages or more. Creating scenes means finding ways for your story to show itself, rather than ways for you to *tell* it.

IS IT A FAIR FIGHT?

Your story's scenes are going to be the specific stages by which your main character's motivations are enacted against opposition, internal or external or both. A motivation against no opposition is boring. How somebody always got everything he wanted, succeeded in every task, won every girl in sight, and never met a comeuppance, wouldn't have any drama. A chronicle of Don Juan's amorous exploits would be dull (even if pornographically dull) without the avenging paternal statue to send the don gibbering off to a well-deserved damnation.

Likewise, opposition without determined contrary motivation, pure victimization, is not only dull, but depressing. This is true even when, as with Oedipus and with Romeo and Juliet, the protagonist's motivation ultimately ends in tragedy or unsuccess. The protagonist of Lovecraft's "The Shadow Over Innsmouth" may end up becoming a part of the horror he tried to escape; Ahab may be the victim of the White Whale he so desired to destroy; but each fought all the way through the shadows into the eventual dark.

A narrative of Dracula's slaughters during the centuries before he met his determined and ultimately successful adversaries, Van Helsing and the thoroughly modern Mina, would be about as engrossing as feeding time at the zoo. Dracula is pure appetite, and his victims merely food, if there is no involving battle between predator and prey. Incidentally, Ann Rice's effective reinventions of the vampire legends (the series *The Vampire Chronicles*) concentrate on the aspirations of the vampires themselves as individuals, and dwell very little on the neck-biting or on their victims. The resulting stories, because the vampires are the protagonists, tend to be surprisingly upbeat in spite of the implied body count.

Bambi Meets Godzilla: *a Cautionary Tale*

Some of you may have seen or heard about a short satirical film called *Bambi Meets Godzilla*. While the opening credits are rolling, we see the terminally cute little fawn nibbling and gamboling in a leafy clearing. Then a big reptilian foot comes down and squashes him. Splat. End of movie. It's startling and funny, in a gruesome sort of way, the first time. But a whole hour of build-up, followed by that expressive splat? A whole novel, even? It would be dreadful.

Anytime you're tempted to write a pure-victim story, in which the protagonist doesn't have a chance, think about *Bambi Meets Godzilla* and try something else.

An Even Battle Is More Fun to Watch

Whether the ending is happy or unhappy in the traditional sense, any story needs to be founded on an effective and strongly-felt conflict, in which the opposing forces—whether people, ideas, attitudes, or a mix—are at least fairly evenly matched, enough so that the final outcome is in doubt. If anything, the forces opposing the protagonist ought to seem the stronger, to create drama and suspense. But not an utter mismatch.

Oedipus was doomed from the beginning; but he didn't know it, and he was fighting all the way. The emphasis was on the fighting, not on the doom. That's what makes the fighting, the wrestling, become engrossing narrative.

It's been said that happy families don't make good stories. Only unhappy families, or people who for whatever reason are discontented with their current circumstances, give rise to good fiction. If Scarlett O'Hara had easily forgotten Ashley and been rapturously married to an easily domesticated Rhett Butler early in the novel, if the Civil War hadn't intruded to complicate their unvarying domestic bliss, if their child had grown happily into adolescence and beyond, who would want to read *Gone With the Wind*?

Struggle, conflict, dissatisfaction, aspiration, choice: these are the basis of effective plots.

HOW TO TEST A STORY IDEA

If you're like most of the writers I've run into, you have more story ideas than you know what to do with. They're popping into your mind faster than you can jot them down in your handy bedside notebook.

And how could it be otherwise? Things have been happening to you, and to everybody you know, all your life. You've been reading, and absorbing stories, almost that long. The newspapers and the evening news offer conflicts galore, and memorable people, events of apparent importance. Once you've been writing awhile, people will start forcing stories on you, claiming that they were always going to write them themselves but somehow never got the time. They'll insist the stories are just the thing for your next fiction, and you may even agree with them.

There is no shortage of story ideas that might even *become* stories in the right hands.

Truman Capote took a news account of a brutal and apparently senseless multiple murder and developed it into the nonfiction novel, *In Cold Blood*. Mary Shelley's *Frankenstein* was reportedly based on an alarmingly vivid dream. I took a speculation on the nature of emotion, combined it with some unpleasant childhood memories, and found in the mix the basis for a five-book science fiction series.

Story ideas are everywhere. Finding ideas isn't the problem.

Your problem is every writer's problem: figuring out which, of this barrage of fragmentary ideas, is a potential story; and, even more difficult, a story *you* care about and can tell well.

There are four basic questions you should ask of any new story idea you come up with to decide whether or not it's ready to be developed, or whether it needs to mature awhile longer in your notebook.

1. Is It Your Story to Tell?

All ideas can't become stories *for you*. I could no more write a story about magic than I could sprout wings, or roots. I've realized that, on some fundamental level, I don't believe in magic. Although I heartily enjoy reading stories about witches and occult happenings, I can't really imagine magic and don't take it seriously, not with the fundamental seriousness needed to write convincingly.

I'm interested, I'm willing to play that game with another writer for awhile; but I don't *really care*. Not about magic, anyway.

And most of the ideas that come to you, from whatever source, are going to be like that. They won't be things of profound importance to *you*. And if they're not, how are you going to persuade a reader to care about them? It will all be forced, mechanical, intellectualized, unconvincing. That's even more true if they are things you uncomfortably think you *ought* to care about, like cruel parents, faithless lovers, The Bomb, World Hunger, or the Heartbreak of Psoriasis.

I think that's what the traditional advice to "write what you know" really means: to choose things that matter enormously to you, things you have a stake in settling, at least on paper.

I've never been aboard a spaceship, but I've lived in cramped quarters, and I can project an experience I've known on one I've only imagined. So I can honestly say that I know what it *could* be like to be the sole crew of a one-man scout ship traveling on a long haul between the stars. And I care how it would feel: it seems worth trying to imagine myself into. I've never been a serious sculptor, but I know something of the way any artist can get lost in his work—perfectly normal, experienced from the inside, but often laughably odd, observed from the outside. So I was able to write, with conviction, a story about a sculptor who carves bas-relief horses out of botched tombstones she calls "meat" and who loses track of the hours and even the days.

I'm not saying that these were the most wonderful story ideas ever concocted, just that they were *my* stories to tell. They had a special resonance. I could imagine my way into them, from things I've known about, first-hand. And they had a dynamic: they seemed to be going somewhere from the first moment they came into my head. They felt as if they had little hooks built in that refused to let go until I had the whole puzzle solved, the thing written in the form it seemed to want to go into.

Most often these valid, dynamic story ideas won't be things

that you already know and have settled. Settled things make for explanations, not for absorbing fiction. Instead, they'll be situations or people or memories that are troubling you, things you want, for yourself, to work out and understand. Explorations, not explanations.

That's the first criterion: *Is this something I really care about, something I partly understand, something that seems to want working out?*

2. Is It Too Personal for Readers to Become Involved With?

The second criterion has to do with the purpose of writing. Partly, it's self-expression. But partly—and increasingly, the more and the longer you write—it's communication. You want what you say to reach, and move, a reader. You want to share the exploration. You want to have fun writing your story so that readers can have fun reading it. Maybe you even want it to sell, and to help you become famous. Those are valid reasons too, provided they're not the main or the only ones. (If the results are more important to you than the process, if you don't want to write but only *to have written*, you're in trouble.)

So the second thing you need to ask yourself, about any story idea, is whether it's something that's *too* personal, something that's very important to you but would justifiably bore a stranger sitting next to you on a cross-country bus.

Some experience is too close to us. We feel deep emotion about it, but haven't digested it yet and aren't able to put it in perspective for somebody else to view. Or maybe it's too exotic, like a specialist on the intimate habits of the Amazonian tree snail assuming the subject is going to be fascinating to vast numbers of people.

Personal blind spots.

It's understandable, if mildly tedious, from people waving around pictures of their kids or wanting us to pore through snapshots from their vacations or sit through their home movies of the family washing the dog. From a writer, it's unforgivable—and probably unpublishable.

For such highly personal subjects, the context that would make them meaningful would just take too much explaining for somebody else to understand.

That's a particular problem, by the way, with autobiographical or fact-based fiction. You have to be able to distance it. You not only have to care about it but care just the right way, ruthlessly cutting this incident, changing this character, altering this reaction in the interests of good fiction, regardless of what *really* happened. You have to be, in some meaningful sense, *free* of it before you're ready to write about it. You have to be willing to look at it through a stranger's eyes—the eyes of your potential readers.

But don't underestimate your own experiences as a source of story ideas, either. Tiny, vivid impressions—the feel of new sneakers, sunlight through a colored window, getting up in the middle of the night when it's dark and scary, being the only pedestrian on an empty street—have been the basis of wonderful, imaginative short stories by Ray Bradbury. Coveting an overcoat was the basis of a classic story by Gogol. A chickenwire costume can be life-saving armor. Small things can have immense impact, if you give them a context that brings out their importance.

Your own experience is an inexhaustible mine of fiction ideas, provided only that you can make readers see the experience as important and applicable to their own lives.

You can never know this for sure. You can only recognize the problem and do your best to strike a balance between the personal and the universal. After that, the story has to take its chances, as all stories must.

And always bring, to whatever you write, everything you've known, felt, experienced, imagined. Like Tolkien's Elves of Lorien, put something of what you love in everything you make. If you're cynical or want to escape sentimentality, put in something that you loathe, too. Such first-hand direct experience is the main and invaluable source of the kind of immediately convincing, personal, vivid details that flesh out a plot and make it seem real to a reader.

Dickens, in particular, was a master of this. Joseph Heller's

Catch-22 is another good source for precisely observed detail. Read some of these authors' work and learn the kind of specific detail you should be observing in daily life and jotting in your notebook for later use in fiction—a face, a phrase, a scene. Sometimes the simplest, most personal things are those that can speak direct to the heart.

And the job of distinguishing between the merely personal and the vividly personal is one nobody can do but you.

So your second criterion should be: *Can I work with this idea in a caring but uncompromising way to make it meaningful to somebody else?*

3. Is It Going Somewhere?

The third criterion has to do with the nature of the material itself. Supposing the first two criteria have been met, is this an idea with a dynamic? Has it got an engine, or could you put one into it? You could attach a motor to a tree, but it wouldn't go very far. A motor-powered bathtub is still a bathtub.

Does your idea divide itself into a vivid opening, one or more specific developments, and a solid ending? Can you block out in your mind a beginning scene, intermediate scenes, a final confrontation or resolution of some kind?

It doesn't matter if the actual scenes you end up writing are different from the ones you imagine at first. The important thing is that the subject you care about, the subject you think you can make immediate and important to readers, lends itself to being cast into scenes of any kind.

Make a poster and put it up where you write: PLOT IS A VERB.

If what you're writing is nounish or adjectival, a thing or a description, or if it's essentially a lecture or an essay, it's going to be static. It may still be a story, but a relatively formless one aimed at a narrow spectrum of readers. (Nonplot methods of storytelling will be discussed in Chapter 11.) If your story happens over a period of years, with nothing much happening in between, and if you can't see a way to compress the action into a single compact tale, even one as long as a novel, you'll have to split out a smaller piece of it to be your story. If it involves a vast number of people or several major changes of locale, it may be a novel, but not a short story. If it's all beginning, a problem you can show but not resolve to give the story a conclusion (even an unhappy one), it's not going to work. If it's a sudden turn of events that nothing seems to lead into, like lightning in the middle of a bullfight, pure ending, it won't make satisfying reading.

Ask yourself, *Can I dramatize this in a series of scenes with a minimum of explanation? Does it have a plot, or can I create a plot for it?*

4. What's at Stake?

Finally, ask yourself: *Is there something quite specific and vital at stake—not just to me, but to one or more of the characters involved?* Ask yourself what the central conflict is, the struggle that's the basis of plot. Ask yourself how you can *show*, rather than tell, why this is so important to the character, make the reader understand, empathize, and care about what happens.

If you're writing experimental or literary fiction, you can allow yourself a little more latitude about what's at stake. It can be the impact of a memory of aesthetic ecstasy experienced in a time of artistic dryness, as in Thomas Mann's *Death in Venice*. It can be the downward progress of a deteriorating, obsessive consciousness, as in Poe's "The Fall of the House of Usher." That it's harder to make such things seem vital issues to the general reader doesn't mean they're not worth doing. But neither does it mean that you can ignore the issue and just have meandering ruminations about Life and the World.

It's quite possible to make bread with something other than crushed grain and produce food that's tasty, nutritious, and solid enough so that you know you've eaten something. But whatever your fondness for carrot cake or corn muffins, it's plain old bread, plot, that's been part of human culture since the beginnings of things. We know plot when we meet it: it's in our bones. Maybe even in our genes. We say, "But what's it *about*?" and expect a reasonably concise answer. We want verb bread or we're sure we'll be hungry an hour later.

Any fiction, however literary, still has to possess some dynamic tension, even if it's one of irony, or a surprising contrast. Something has to be seen to matter, and to change—even in a mood piece. The story has to move. If you choose not to have traditional plot, you're going to have to work twice as hard to make your chosen alternate work as compellingly.

If, however, you're writing mainstream or genre fiction intended for a wide readership, it's absolutely crucial that you have and develop a plot and that something quite concrete and definite be at issue. It's what your story is going to be perceived to be "about." Your protagonist wants to gain possession of a ruby approximately the size of New Jersey, become a first-class hockey player, escape from an unsympathetic spouse, get one word of praise from a stern and disapproving parent, or rescue turtles from the zoo and set them free in the all-forgiving sea.

Ideally, you should be able to express the core plot in a sentence or two, in about the same space and style as program listings in *TV Guide*. In fact, it might help to study a few issues of *TV Guide* and one of the several paperback guides to movies on TV, and see how such capsule summaries are done. Practice writing a few about things you've read recently. ("The police chief of a New England vacation community, although terrified of the ocean, sets out to destroy a huge killer shark"—*Jaws*; "A group of British schoolboys, attempting to survive after their plane crashlands on a tropical island, begin reverting to savagery"—*Lord of the Flies*.)

See how brief and direct you can make your summaries. The basic plot of a story (unlike its meaning) ought to be directly expressible in very few words, though playing it out in scenes may take a dozen or a thousand pages.

If the summary of your own story turns out to be one you haven't already seen fifty times, so much the better. If not, don't worry: all the love stories haven't yet been written, nor anything close. And there will be growing-up stories as long as there are people. Some topics, handled in a fresh way, are inexhaustible.

READY, STEADY, GO!

If you test your ideas against these four criteria, a lot will be tossed out, or saved in your handy notebook for later. Don't let that upset you. There are a lot more where they came from, and some of them will pass the test with bells ringing and flags flying.

All you need is one solid story idea at a time to keep writing productively, successfully, your whole life. Use these criteria and you'll have the confidence of knowing you're starting with good material from the very beginning, material worth the thought and energy of developing, stories that have the potential of reaching readers. You'll hardly be able to wait to start working out your ideas on paper, embodying them in scenes, listening to your characters talk.

Don't wait.

Start now.

CHAPTER 2

GRAND OPENINGS

YOU HAVE A STORY IDEA. You've tested it with the four questions to make sure it's basically sound. You've decided whether it seems to want to be long or short fiction. Now you're going to have to people and dramatize it. How do you start?

The first thing to realize is that generally you're *not* going to begin at the beginning. Your story's start, the actual words that begin the narrative, will be a good way along in the progress of the events you're imagining.

The Greeks, as translated by the Romans, called it *in medias res*: in the middle of things. Starting there, in the middle of things, is even more necessary if your story is going to have negative motivation—that is, if it's one in which your chief character, the protagonist, is reacting against something that has happened. Stories arising from reactions have a past that will try to encumber the story's beginning, if you let it.

That kind of built-in past is called 'exposition'—the necessary explanations that are needed to understand what's going on *now*. Because exposition is, of its nature, telling rather than showing, it's intrinsically less dramatic than a scene. So it needs careful handling.

Maybe you're thinking, Well, I'll avoid the problem of handling exposition by going back to the very beginning of things, when the people involved first met, before there were any problems between them, so there will be no need of background material.

NO!

I say "No" so strongly because exposition very seldom makes good plot. It turns into an explanation. Nothing is happening. Long stretches of exposition tend to get boring very, very fast. I'll talk in more detail about handling exposition in Chapter 4. For now, know that however you handle it, you should do everything possible to avoid encumbering your beginnings with it.

Departure from a Norm

If what you're trying to show is a change from a pre-existing norm (contrasting before/after or then/now), and that norm is really vital to what is going to happen, you should demonstrate that norm in the briefest possible space, as something already being departed from. A paragraph or two, at most, in a short story; a page or two, in a novel. And neither paragraph nor page should generally be the first one. Get your action rolling *first*, then back off to show the normal state of things.

That's what Dickens does, in *A Christmas Carol*. It starts out, "Marley was dead to begin with." Then we move to an overview of what's normal for Scrooge—his coldly businesslike attitudes, his harshness and callousness—in a series of brief confrontations with his nephew, with businessmen collecting for charity, and with his clerk, Bob Cratchit. His attitudes are all the more shocking in that this isn't just any ordinary day, but Christmas Eve. Then, when Scrooge shuts up shop and goes home, he sees the face of his dead ex-partner, Marley, on his door-knocker and things get rapidly stranger from then on.

The plot gets rolling before Dickens backs off and gives the norm—Scrooge's pre-existing attitudes. This norm isn't explained but instead is demonstrated, shown in a series of brief scenes, after which Dickens returns to the main plot, Scrooge's confrontation with his own past, present, and grim probable future, as embodied by the tortured wraith of Marley, Scrooge's mirror. (More on mirrors and other methods of echoing the main action in Chapter 8.)

You can even set up a character to represent the norm. That's the function Watson serves in the Holmes stories, and the average Ralph as contrasted with ambitious Jack, fat incompetent clever Piggy, and mystical Simon in *Lord of the Flies*. Such a character gives the reader somebody to identify with and judge the other, more unusual characters by.

My strong advice is that if establishing a pre-existing norm isn't absolutely vital, skip it. Leave it out altogether, if you possibly can. Instead, start *in medias res*. In general practice, that means starting your actual narrative just before, or even during, the first major conflict or confrontation: the point at which things start to get serious, when they start moving toward final crisis.

Specifically, that means starting a short story *just before* the main crisis which will provide the story's resolution. Start a novel *during* the first crisis, because you'll have time to draw back and explain how things got that way later in the first chapter, or even in chapter two.

Don't tell how the protagonist decided to go out and buy fireworks, how much they cost, how he brought them home, how he stored them, what his wife said. Begin when the fuse is lit and the reader sees a bang coming any minute.

JUGGLING THREE BALLS AT ONCE

Every effective beginning needs to do three things. The chief of these is to get the story going and show what kind of story it's going to be. The second is to introduce and characterize the protagonist. The third is to engage the reader's interest in reading on.

Some beginnings do more than this. Some create moods; some introduce narrators who aren't the protagonist, or one or more of the subordinate characters. Some, as just discussed, establish a norm the story will then depart from.

A story can do more than these three things; but it should never do less.

These three special jobs are absolutely vital. To the degree that any short story or novel neglects them, it's risking being dull, uninvolving and possibly confusing reading.

Remember, I'm talking about the *very beginning* here: the first page or so of a short story, the first few pages of a novel.

Setting the Scene with a Scene

The most economical way of handling these three jobs is to find some way of doing all three at once.

And the best way of doing that, generally, is inventing an appropriate scene: what's going on when the reader starts your story.

Try to think up what situation your protagonist could be in which would directly lead into the final crisis or confrontation, whatever it's going to be. Not an idea, not a description: a situation. A dramatized action with some kind of inherent conflict appropriate to what will follow. The opening situation should be true to the story as a whole, not be (or seem) something tacked on just for the sake of a vivid, exciting opening which, in retrospect, will seem contrived.

Look at the opening of Stephen King's *It*. A child dies, dragged down a grate during a rainstorm by what appears to be a malevolent clown looking up from the sewer. The threat isn't a fake—a child can die, the beginning tells us. And since the rest of the novel involves children trying to understand and defeat the threat that "clown" poses, the opening is valid to the rest of the book. It makes a reader interested in reading on, to learn how this murderous menace will be fought. And it characterizes the protagonist in a brief scene where he makes the paper boat which the boy (the protagonist's little brother) was chasing when the clown got him.

It's an opening which does all its necessary jobs well.

Characters Busy Being Themselves Before Our Very Eyes

Next, think what your protagonist could be doing, in the context of that situation, which would directly show, with little or no explanation from you, exactly what kind of person he or she is.

In the beginning of *Lord of the Flies*, Ralph finds a conch shell on the beach. Piggy comments on how valuable such shells are and tells Ralph a conch can be blown, like a trumpet. Piggy, being asthmatic, can't blow the shell himself; but his information is what allows Ralph to blow the shell, calling the scattered castaway boys together for the first time.

That shell is the emblem of leadership through the rest of the book. Ralph, finder of the shell, is the leader as long as the shell lasts, with Piggy as his "brain trust"—precisely the pattern set up at the book's opening. When the conch is destroyed, the shell and Piggy both smashed by a huge boulder rolled by Jack's chief henchman, the action represents the destruction of any authority save that of power and of fear. Piggy is dead. The reader knows that the hunt for Ralph won't be long in coming.

Again, this is a masterly beginning in which each character, upon entering, does something that economically and effectively *shows* precisely who and what he is, in this particular context.

And notice how the conch is used to characterize the people who come in contact with it. It becomes a symbol, not because the author arbitrarily assigned some significance to it by a species of novelistic footnote, but because that object has a particular, strong, and important meaning to the people associated with it. The meaning is intrinsic within the story, validly part of the object itself. Even if your objects are less emotionally charged than the conch, or than that novel's later talismanic object, a pig's head rotting on a pole, you can still use them effectively. A man carrying an umbrella is different from a man *not* carrying an umbrella, when an author chooses (and invents) his details carefully and with absolute economy.

Props and Settings

Give your character objects to be associated with, to carry, to use. In acting, they're called props, and I'll call them that too. Well chosen, well used, props can demonstrate some essential truth about a character without the need of blocks of description slowing down the pace. Think how King uses the paper boat in the opening of *It*, or Golding's conch. Think of the raft in *Huckleberry Finn*, the much sought-after black bird in Hammett's *The Maltese Falcon*. A good prop is a kind of visual shorthand and, like a picture, it can be worth a thousand words, especially at a story's beginning.

And the same thing is true, for the same reasons, about settings. They aren't just backdrops. Just by where you have the action happening will tell a lot about the action itself and the people involved. A scene on a rainy street corner is automatically different from one in a hot, stuffy and claustrophobic schoolroom, or at a county fair, or in an echoing, empty parking garage. You can reinforce the mood and action with your choice of setting, or work against it: a grim thing happening on a carousel, a happy thing happening beside a car nose-down in a ditch. Wherever you set your opening, be aware that where it happens matters, and can matter enormously, if the setting is well chosen to complement or contrast with what's happening there.

It may take thinking over to come up with good props, vivid, meaningful settings. Be ready to think twice, try and discard, until everything seems to be working together in one seemingly inevitable whole with nothing extra and nothing missing.

Don't Bog Your Opening Down in Descriptions

Have your characters enter talking and doing, in a significant and characteristic way. It doesn't matter when, if ever, you get around to telling what they look like. Some stories do descriptions in just a few sketched details—Sam Spade's "satanic" V of eyebrows, for instance—and some never find it necessary at all: describe Huckleberry Finn. Can you do it? Twain doesn't. Perry Mason, in the numerous novels featuring his wily court maneuvers, doesn't look at all like Raymond Burr: Erle Stanley Gardner deliberately refrained from describing him. Nor does Robert Parker find it necessary to tell more about his private detective, Spenser, than that he's strongly built and well past thirty.

Sometimes the most important thing about a person isn't how he looks, but what he's like, how he behaves, how and what he thinks, how he reacts, even how he talks. Huck Finn, and the characters in Damon Runyon's flavorful short stories, are characterized almost completely by means of their voices—their inimitably slangy way of speaking. Appearance (meaning the kind of crude color-of-hair, color-of-eyes, height/weight/age "police-blotter listing") may not be important at all.

Piggy's weight, asthma, and glasses are crucially important

in the story, and so are carefully detailed. The color of his hair, by contrast, makes no difference at all.

Only spend time describing what it's *important* to describe, what's going to matter in the rest of the story. That may be what your characters look like; then again, it may not. You decide.

And even if your characters' appearance *is* important to you and your story, the story's very beginning may not be the best place to go into any great detail about it. You want your readers to be able to imagine your characters, not describe them for a robbery report. Have your people talking and doing: that will make the stronger impression.

Opening with a Bang

Some openings are unabashedly melodramatic. Their action is as violent, exaggerated, and mindless as possible. "As I scrambled over the top of the crater, Mount St. Helens cleared its throat and then blew 200,000 tons of its substance straight into the startled sky." Let's call them *volcano openings*. (In Chapter 10, I'll talk about the other half of the equation, *dirigible endings*.)

A volcano opening—a chase scene, somebody falling off a cliff or being attacked by Killer Shrews, a sex scene or mad, passionate love-at-first-sight—makes a statement about what's to follow. The story, such an opening says, is going to be one of exaggerated nonstop action/emotion, lots of excitement and suspense, intended to appeal to the broadest possible spectrum of readers. If you can make good on a promise like that, you could have a best-seller on your hands, and movie rights in the offing.

Assuming that's what you want. . . .

That's one sure thing about a volcano: it gets your attention. But it's also a hard act to follow. And not all writers want to. While some writers yearn for the primary colors and broad sweep of Cinemascope, others have a hankering for the small screen, muted tones, and close ups.

If you don't intend to have a slam-bang action story or scenery-chewing, bodice-ripping forbidden romance following an opening like that, it would have been better to have made a little less noise at the outset and, instead, made a different sort of promise. You could promise an unusual concept ("Big Brother is Watching": *1984*), an especially vivid character (Sherlock Holmes), or maybe an interesting, individual style ("It was love at first sight. The first time Yossarian saw the chaplain he fell madly in love with him": *Catch-22*).

The point is that if you're beginning a short story or novel, you are in fact making a promise the rest of the story will have to fulfill. You don't have any choice about that, because the beginning is, by definition, what gets read first. A reader (and an editor considering publishing it) is going to decide whether or not to read on, based on what that beginning promises. It has to promise something special, or something seen in a special way, to make them want to read on.

And, remember, I'm talking now just about beginnings, not whole plots. Exaggerated events and people are a staple even in literary fiction. Virtually everything by Faulkner has large doses of melodrama—take a look at *Sanctuary*, for instance. The melodrama compensates for Faulkner's characteristically involuted, complex prose style and considerable stretches of philosophizing. So-called Southern Gothic, whether penned by Faulkner or Carson McCullers, has a native streak of the bizarre all through it—freaks, dwarfs, mouldering bodies of old lovers in upstairs bedrooms.

Steinbeck's *East of Eden* and *Of Mice and Men* have adulteries and murders and hard-breathing domestic hanky-panky galore. Dickens' novels have melodrama by the ton. And all are certainly regarded as literature.

But if you look at the beginnings of any of these, you'll find the tone rather quiet, the situations revealing but not characterized by slam-bang action. The melodrama comes later. Virtually no volcano openings.

Better, for hooking the reader, is a *revealing* opening, effectively played out, promising something worth watching to come. Better is something relatively simple and direct, free of encumbering description, explanation, and hype, something a reader can understand immediately by just watching, a situation able to speak for itself. A parent with a hand raised, and a child grimly swallowing tears; a middle-aged woman anxiously scanning the want ads, answering inattentively as a teenager asks when supper is going to be ready; a man and woman stiffly silent or talking about everything except abortion as they wait for a train, as in Hemingway's wonderful "The Hills Like White Elephants."

Find the right scene, one that hits just the right note with a minimum of fuss, and the beginning will take care of itself.

And if it leads to melodrama later on, so be it. You and your story will certainly be in the best of literary company. In Chapter 7, I'll offer some tips on harnessing the fierce power of melodrama to narrative purposes.

Do You Always Have to Make a Scene?

Scene openings aren't the only way. They're just the simplest, most reliable way, suitable for any kind of writing. If you're just starting to write, they're probably what you should use for your beginnings.

But there are alternatives. Good stories have begun with pure dialogue. Dickens' *A Tale of Two Cities* begins with a philosophical overview: "It was the best of times, it was the worst of times" and his *Bleak House* opens with a wonderful portrait of dense fog spreading through London the same way the foggy intricacies of the case Jarndyce vs. Jarndyce spread to obscure and pollute everything and everyone they touch. Steinbeck's masterpiece, *The Grapes of Wrath*, begins with a splendid description of a dust storm. Du Maurier's *Rebecca* begins, "Last night I dreamt I went to Manderley again," calling up the image of that doomed house.

If you begin with something other than a scene, you'll have to compensate for the loss of immediate action by using something especially striking and powerful. Starting with a description, a philosophical mini-essay, or a dream is dangerous because all will tend to be essentially static if you don't go to heroic lengths to make them something else.

They'll sit and look at you like a fried egg. Your story will stall.

Strong contrast or a strikingly unusual juxtaposition (implied comparison between a law case and a fog, for instance), vivid imagery or wording, a violent or melodramatic event being described, a brooding mood that promises action soon to come—all can help give the reader a *sense* of motion even when nothing is actually happening *right now.*

But such openings are difficult to bring off, and unless your alternative method of opening can somehow contrive to do the required three jobs of all beginnings, your best choice will be a scene.

IF AT FIRST IT DOESN'T START, START AGAIN

Now if all this discussion makes a beginning sound crucial and complicated, it is. But then, so are middles. So are endings.

If you have a story idea, then don't worry about the beginning. Get your story told, all the way through, at least in first draft.

As I've said before, stories change in the telling. Often you'll find that what you thought was going to be the heart of the story ends up as kind of an appendix, and the story's true motion and true meaning have gone someplace you never expected. And if and when that happens, the original beginning (if you had one) is going to be the wrong beginning anyway. It will need rethinking, re-imagining.

The Dirty Word

Now I'm going to use a dirty word. Otherwise strong writers shudder and flinch when they hear it.

REVISION.

Any story worth the telling is worth revising. Remember Melville's Bulkington, who fell overboard the first night out of port? If you have such vestigial evidence of a false beginning, be tidier than Melville: go back and change it. Make your story one single solid thing, itself, with nothing left that could stand to be omitted without weakening it, nothing omitted or left sketchy that really needs to be developed for the story to have its proper impact.

Don't assume first thoughts are always best thoughts. Second thoughts, about something already well along in the process of becoming, are often better, more insightful thoughts because they're about something concrete—*this* short story, *this* novel—instead of something vague and theoretical, a set of intentions, a blur of feelings not yet fleshed out into a complex of incident and personality.

Be thinking about your opening, but don't worry about it. If it doesn't come, or come to life, right away, skip over it and write the next scene with just a few notes on what you want the beginning to have done and established, what groundwork it will have laid, for what comes afterward, the part you're working on now. And keep writing away until you have one whole first draft done. Then go ahead and start the kind of invention, addition, and deletion only possible in solid second-draft writing.

I don't know if William Golding knew he was going to need a conch when he began writing *Lord of the Flies*. It's altogether possible that, realizing how important some tangible, visible symbol of leadership was becoming in the story's middle, he went back and stuck the conch on that beach for Ralph to find and for Piggy to identify. Be ready to do the same, once your story has started talking to you and letting you know what *it* needs, instead of what you thought it was going to need.

In other words, a bad beginning shouldn't be the end—not if you realize you'll often need to go back and write it all over anyway, even when you initially thought you got it right the first time around.

CHAPTER 3

WOULD YOU TRUST A VIEWPOINT WITH SHIFTY EYES?

WHILE YOU'RE WRITING YOUR OPENING and then going on into the beginning of your story, you'll need to settle two things right away:

Whose viewpoint is going to control the storytelling?

How are you going to fit in (or manage to leave out) background information if, as I've advised, you've begun in the middle?

I can only talk about one of these at a time, but pretend I'm talking about both at once, because both need to be decided at the same time, namely right away. This chapter is on some fundamental choices regarding viewpoint. The next one is on handling exposition.

HOW MANY EYES ARE ENOUGH?

Sometimes there's no viewpoint character, nobody whose eyes focus the action. Instead, the author tells the story. That's called omniscient (all-knowing) narration. The author narrates, mentioning what this or that character may be feeling or thinking anytime the author pleases.

The trouble with using an omniscient narrator is that all the characters are kept at arm's length, seen equally and from a distance. It tends to be uninvolving. A reader finds it harder to identify with any one character, since the focus and the viewpoint range over all equally.

Unfocused sunlight won't set fire to a piece of paper. It takes a magnifying glass, a single focus, to do that.

So although current fiction may use omniscience in an inconspicuous, sometime way, in the form of narrative summary or other brief, transitional elements, thoroughgoing omniscient narration is now seldom used as the controlling viewpoint of a whole short story (with a few notable exceptions like John Cheever's short fiction), and even more rarely of a novel.

Instead of adopting a broad-focus omniscient narrative voice to be the controlling viewpoint of a whole story, contemporary writers and readers seem to prefer something more like our own experience, in which each of us can know—but not always understand—the inner life of only one person: ourselves. Everybody else is seen from the outside, and known only by what they say and do, and what we think about it. Mirroring our individual experience in fiction means having one central viewpoint character and sticking with him or her.

In short fiction, a single viewpoint character has always been most common, though there are quite a lot of exceptions. Longer short stories, those shading toward novelette length, sometimes will have two or more viewpoint characters. The brevity of short fiction is, naturally enough, the determining factor in whether a given story will support more than one viewpoint without losing impact and immediacy.

But long fiction has space to develop several characters in depth. Intensity rises and falls as the story progresses. Novels also sometimes need to shift locale or show scenes where it would be impractical or impossible for the protagonist to be present, yet which the author doesn't want to relegate to reports or summaries. Or sometimes a writer wants to build suspense by switching the narrative focus from the main plot to a subplot ("Meanwhile, back at the ranch—") or reveal some fact to the reader, yet keep the main character ignorant of it.

In those cases, having just one viewpoint character may be

impractical, even undesirable. So in novels, multiple viewpoints are as common as single focus.

Winning Reader Identification

The danger of multiple viewpoints is that the reader, lacking just one person to identify with, is likely to become more a detached, uninvolved observer and less a vicarious participant in your story's events. The story, seen piecemeal through several different sets of eyes, may become disconnected, confusing, and incoherent, especially if it contains any other kind of complexity, like flashbacks, many extreme changes of locale, or an intricate or subplot-laden plot.

A story with too many focuses can become a story with no focus at all.

Using a single viewpoint character is the best way to communicate excitement, dread, love, any strong emotion, to the reader, make readers share the feeling and not just the facts your story presents. It's easier to imagine your way into a single character, one on one, than into several in succession.

To the degree you're trying to arouse or communicate emotions in your story, you need to involve your reader; and that means doing everything possible to help your reader identify with the main person that story is about.

Winning that kind of intense reader identification means using the fewest possible viewpoints. If there are no compelling reasons to do otherwise, stay with one viewpoint character from beginning to end. If you really need two, use two. If you can't do without three, then use three. But fight, if you have to, to keep from making it seven or seventeen. Keep it to the absolute minimum.

SINGLE VIEWPOINT: WHOSE EYES ARE BEST?

If you've decided to use a single viewpoint character, the main choice, the one to depart from only for good reason, is telling the story from the viewpoint of the chief character, the protagonist. He or she is the one the story's events are centered around. He or she is the one who's going to be chiefly affected by what happens.

But don't forget: the protagonist is whoever *you say* the protagonist is; that choice, in turn, determines the nature of the whole story. The story of a flood is a different story if it's told from the point of view of Ginger, a drenched mother clinging to a chimney with five children and an irritated cat, waiting for rescue, than if it's told from the point of view of Fred, her equally drenched husband, a volunteer fireman in a rowboat who is quite content to rescue people on the other side of town and is rather hoping to find himself an unencumbered bachelor again.

Who is really at the story's heart? It may not have been the character you first assumed it was. If you're having trouble with the story of Ginger and Fred and you've been telling it from Ginger's viewpoint, maybe it's really Fred's story and you hadn't noticed. Try looking at the story through another character's eyes—the man in the rowboat instead of the woman on the roof—and see if it makes a better, more satisfying story that way.

Or if it's the story of Ginger and Fred but they're both bores, maybe it's ten-year-old Tiffany's story. Except that Tiffany doesn't yet exist. You have to invent her.

After a story is written, it's hard to imagine it could be otherwise than the way it is. But when you're writing it, all the choices are yours—even, and especially, the one of whose story it is and whose eyes would be best to see it. Because who sees determines in large measure what gets seen: what happens and how it's told about.

Holmes and Heathcliff: an Outsider's View

A displaced viewpoint character, a narrator other than the main character, is an option. Generally it's used when the writer doesn't want the reader to get too close to the protagonist, maybe to keep the main character strange and mysterious. That's the case, I think, in Fitzgerald's *The Great Gatsby*. The man who called himself Jay Gatsby is full of secrets and private romantic dreams;

Nick Carraway, the narrator, is an onlooker and a thoughtful, moral man. Fitzgerald wanted the story seen by the wise man, not by the dreamer. He wanted to put a filter, a barrier, between Gatsby and the reader, to keep Gatsby a distant figure seen only from and through Carraway's perspective.

Emily Bronte's *Wuthering Heights* also uses displaced narration, partly for the same reason—to emphasize the narrators' rationalism rather than the wild, mystical romanticism of the main characters, Heathcliff and Catherine. But in this book, something else is operating too. You may have a protagonist who's cruel, savage, or hard to understand or like, as Heathcliff certainly is. You may have a Sherlock Holmes, who's so uniquely brilliant and so disinclined to explain, that you need a go-between as a narrator, to act as the reader's eyes and to stand for a norm which the main character violates either for good or for evil. The distance between reader and chief character is already there: what's needed is a bridge.

That bridge, that displaced narrator, may be Watson, who's fascinated by Holmes and communicates that fascination to the reader while letting Holmes produce his amazing deductions like rabbits out of hats. It may be Ishmael, letting us observe Ahab's monomania without having to sympathize with or share it. It may be Lockwood, who shares with a gossiping old housekeeper the narrative chore of revealing the mutually destructive love of Heathcliff and Catherine.

If your story has a highly unusual protagonist, using a displaced narrator the reader can more easily understand and identify with, who can ask questions and bring some objectivity to the protagonist's odd goings on, may be the best answer.

MULTIPLE VIEWPOINTS: HOW DO YOU SWITCH?

So. You've thought about it and decided your story really needs to be seen through two or more sets of eyes. How do you manage the switches?

A good rule for doing anything tricky in fiction, particularly long fiction—switching viewpoints or anything else—is to do it right away, to let the reader know the rules, and to do it consistently thereafter.

And make no mistake: viewpoint shifts really *are* tricky to handle and are worth all your craft and care. Badly handled, they're as jarring to most readers (*especially* including editors!) as the feeling you get when you thought there were ten steps and there were only nine. Or, worse, when you thought there were ten, there are eleven, and you take a header.

Mangling viewpoint shifts is one of the sirens-howling signals of an utter beginner—as bad as saying "ain't" in front of your strictest teacher. Worse, maybe. It can land your manuscript right back in your self-addressed, stamped envelope as fast as any other beginner's boner I can think of.

Watch out for careless or unintentional viewpoint shifts and cut them out ruthlessly. Treat needed shifts with the utmost respect, the sort you'd accord a loaded gun.

With Two Characters

If you're going to be switching from Ginger to Fred, there are three main ways to handle the change: scene by scene, chapter by chapter, or part by part.

If you decide to make your switches scene by scene, do your first switch in the first few pages, when one scene changes to another, taking special care that the reader knows the switch has happened. Start the new scene with the new viewpoint and establish it in the very first paragraph with something like, "Ginger was dragging the cat back from the edge of the roof. She . . . ." Then carry on from Ginger's point of view for a *little* while, and switch it back to Fred with a new scene.

Similarly, in long fiction, you may want to have a couple of scene-by-scene shifts in the first chapter to establish the pattern, then go to chapter-by-chapter shifts thereafter.

Whichever you choose, establish the pattern as early as you can. After that, you can stay with Ginger or with Fred more or less as long as you like: you've clued your reader in on the method. There are going to be just two viewpoints, Ginger and Fred, and the story is going to shuttle between them. The reader understands and will bear with you thereafter.

The third way is to have extended sections from each point of view in turn, with no internal switches within sections. In short stories, individual scenes are sometimes grouped into something resembling chapters: these sections are either numbered or otherwise strongly set apart from the rest. Similarly, in long fiction, chapters are sometimes grouped together into larger units, sometimes called parts (for instance, Part I, Part II, etc., but still within the same novel).

If your story is going to have parts, you could have each part told from one point of view, and not change until the next part. With substantial stretches spent in each viewpoint, the danger of confusing the reader would be minimal.

With Two Viewpoints, Watch Out for a Divorce

The problem with alternating viewpoints is that the story may start to split into two unconnected narratives. That's what happens in Thackeray's *Vanity Fair*, with its two protagonists: scheming, fascinating Becky Sharp and teary, helpless, tedious Amelia Sedley. The book breaks in two, and the Amelia portion pales by comparison. To prevent a similar split, you'll need to take special care to connect the two viewpoints and plot lines every now and again. Bring the main characters together periodically. Make connections of objects, or moods, or continuing action to bind one scene to the next, in spite of the viewpoint shift. Have some subordinate characters appear in sections told from each of the viewpoints. Remember that with a divided narrative, you're going to have to compensate with increased strong connective narrative devices, to make sure one viewpoint character doesn't end up hogging the whole story and most of the reader's interest.

Be prepared for the problem your choice creates, and decide how you're going to compensate for it.

With Many Characters

If you're going to have several viewpoint characters, what's called rotating viewpoint, the problem is a little different.

You'll find rotating viewpoint exclusively in long fiction. I can't think of a single short story that uses it, though there's doubtless at least one—there are exceptions, and effective ones, to any general rule, when it comes to fiction. Nevertheless, there's usually just not enough space in short fiction to do that kind of switching without fragmenting the story beyond repair.

You can handle your rotation of narrators more or less the same as you would alternating viewpoint, when only two characters are involved. But in this case, it might be a good idea to spend a little more time developing the future viewpoint characters in earlier chapters, *before* they have to take over the responsibility of narration. Let the reader get to know and be interested in them first, before your whole story's viewpoint is turned over to them. If you establish them well, the reader should be able to shift over with no sense of discontinuity when they take over.

If you want to rotate viewpoints frequently, rather than waiting for chapter or part breaks, you should establish the pattern right away. Do at least three or four shifts, briefly, making each scene as self-contained and self-explanatory as possible. The five little paragraphs that make up Ginger's scene have the considerable job of making Ginger and her immediate situation perfectly clear to the reader. The three paragraphs of Fred's scene have to do the same for Fred. When we get to Tiffany, roosting in a treetop by the elementary school, the reader will understand the pattern.

Separate the scenes within chapters either with extra white space, some sort of graphic (* * *), or both. Don't change viewpoints within a scene.

Build in Connections

You'll remember that earlier in the chapter, I recommended a rule of thumb: if something in a story is complicated, keep everything else as simple and direct as possible. Multiple viewpoints need that kind of compensation, especially at first, or the narrative will fragment and become confusing. So take special care to connect the scenes every way you can think of.

In this hypothetical story of ours, the flood itself could be one such connection. Each little scene, in the beginning of the story, could start with a mention of the water and follow a similar narrative pattern: first water, then the person looking at the water in a particular way, then their immediate situation. (After characters and situations are well established, further along in the story, not so many connections will be needed.)

An additional connection could be one mood which, at that moment, all the viewpoint characters share: they're all frightened, and you're dwelling on the particular *kind* of fright that special person is feeling in his or her individual situation.

Keep to consistency of form, just at first, to compensate for the pogo-stick jumps as much as possible.

You might mention Tiffany in Ginger's piece, and Fred in Tiffany's, to add other connections.

Another Way to Keep Things Simple

Viewpoints shifts are distracting. The jumps, and keeping the different characters straight, are going to be taking all a reader's attention. At a story's beginning, if the little scenes themselves are complex or involve a lot of individualized characters, or even the *names* of a lot of different characters, the reader is going to be utterly lost and give up.

At the beginning of a rotating-viewpoint story (the sort we've been imagining), keep the *plot* of the first few scenes to things you could understand in a thirty-second commercial. Somebody trying to climb up on a higher branch while ugly water laps over her patent-leathers doesn't need a whole lot of explaining. Neither does the cat descending the roof to investigate a squirrel crouched in the rain gutter. Show simple things, vivid things, and let the switches provide the motion and energy to propel the story forward, there at the beginning.

Don't mention the names of any characters who aren't vital to the scene or to the scene immediately following. You can mention Ginger's husband is named Fred if Fred's section comes next, but don't mention the in-laws or the neighbors or Fred's boss if the information isn't absolutely necessary and the characters don't appear *in that scene*. Develop or introduce extra characters later, when the context calls for them and they have something to do. Don't have your entire cast of characters, and all their relationships, cluttering the narrative at the beginning.

This is a good principle even in single-viewpoint stories. Beginnings should avoid clutter in all ways possible.

Make Sure the Reader Knows Something's Happening, and Going to Happen

There's another compensation that needs mentioning. Make sure none of your little, simple scenes is static. End them, subtly or obviously, on cliff-hangers. Show something is slipping, something is going wrong, and something is going to happen *very* soon. That, together with the energy the shifts themselves provide, will supply the dynamic force to make the reader want to keep reading and go to the effort of sorting out all the different people, settings, and situations. Make sure that each scene *moves* and is leading up to something quite clear and concrete.

REMEMBER: YOU CAN CHANGE YOUR MIND

The nice thing about writing is that only the finished product, the final draft, has to be seamless and as nearly perfect as you can make it. The first and intermediate drafts can be scribbled up twenty times, and nobody ever has to know but you.

If you started out with a single viewpoint and want to broaden the focus to other major characters for any compelling reason, build a few shifts into the early sections to prepare, to set the pattern, then go ahead and do your shifts thereafter. If you had several viewpoints but find you end up using only about three, go back and adjust things, assigning the orphaned observations to the chosen characters or to narrative summary.

The basic principle is to use as few viewpoints as you possibly can. If that's seven or seventeen, so be it.

Just don't change your mind in the middle (or, worse, the end!) of a story without doing the necessary tidying and adjustment to make the change fit in.

A case in point: a friend told me recently about a book he'd just read in which the principal character, the viewpoint character, got killed off in the middle of the story. It was quite a wrench, I gather, and rather blunted my friend's enthusiasm for the rest of the book, which concerned an investigation of the startling death. It was certainly an unusual plot twist; but I think I'd feel let down if I encountered it. What do you think?

NEVER IN THE MIDDLE OF A SCENE

Returning now to a point made, briefly, earlier: however many viewpoints you're using—two or several—never never NEVER shift viewpoint in the middle of a scene.

Now, wait before you start yelling you've seen it done. I don't doubt there are instances in published work: you can find examples of any ghastly, incompetent boner you can think of, somewhere or other. Characters change names in mid-story. Protagonists get killed off halfway through. Characters make unconvincing speeches to one another to convey information to readers, or treat us to interminable partisan harangues. Characters peer earnestly into mirrors and inventory their looks as if vaguely fearing their noses might have been stolen. Stories obsessively detail every bite of a meal, every trivial bit of the daily routine of getting up in the morning.

Bad writing, by any standard you care to name, sometimes reaches the printed page.

Print doesn't sanctify it. I've read some really rottenly-written fiction over the years, and not all of it in dog-eared copies with garish covers, from used-book shops—how about you?

But competent writers have their lapses, too. In many cases where a major narrative blunder survives into print, it's tolerated because the story shines like a jewel, flaws and all, and the momentary failure of craft (like the vestiges of Bulkington) is forgiven for the sake of the power of the whole.

Some boners are allowed great writers. Laughably bad technique is often tolerated from very popular writers. But you and I are interested in good craft, in understanding options and making choices on purpose. If you didn't care about craft, you wouldn't be reading this book. So you wouldn't want to cite others' blunders to justify your own anyway—right?

The Prosecution rests.

Therefore. After the beginning of a scene, don't change viewpoint until the scene is over. The next scene can be a continuation of the same action—Ginger on the roof, and little Gertrude, aged 6, also on the roof—but it will have a separate concern, a separate viewpoint, its own miniplot with Gertrude at the center, not her mother. Or it may be a transitional stretch of limited omniscient summary. But in one scene, stay with one viewpoint.

If, for this present scene, you're in Fred's viewpoint, be *very sure* to tell directly only *what Fred himself could reasonably observe and know* about other people. Don't say, in Fred's scene, "Old Mike heard the train whistle." Don't say, "The train whistle told Old Mike the railway embankment, anyway, was above water." *Fred can't know what Old Mike hears*, or what anything tells Mike, train whistles included. Say something more like, "Old Mike cocked his head at the distant hooting of a train. 'Guess the embankment's still above water,' he remarked, smoothing rain out of his mustache."

Don't have characters being happy, or thoughtful, or pleased unless they're specifically *looking* or *sounding* happy, thoughtful, or pleased. Let word choice in dialogue, and expression and gesture, do their proper work. That's what they're for. In Fred's scene, stay absolutely with Fred.

Your narrative's first job, at the beginning of the new scene, is to let the reader know as quickly and economically as possible (1) that the shift has happened and (2) whose eyes he's seeing through now. Don't leave that in doubt a single sentence longer than you have to. Do it right away.

And in second draft, watch out for any unintended shifts and stamp them out like roaches, every one.

THE EYES THAT MATTER

They're *your* eyes, your coherent vision of what you're trying to say and show. Whether you displace that vision into a narrator or have a viewpoint-protagonist who is a thinly disguised version of yourself, the job is the same: to see things whole and clear and true. To focus on what's important and let the unimportant blur or drop out. To be a photographer of the mind, noting how the shadows are cast by your own private inner sun.

In ancient times, it was believed that the eye sent out rays that illuminated and affected whatever was seen. Belief in "the Evil Eye" is a vestige of that ancient concept of the eye's function. For a writer, it's still true, and always has been. You light up what you see, when you embody it in a story. Then others can see it too. Innumerable learned books are written on this or that author's "vision," the unique worlds created by seeing them and writing about them.

That kind of seeing, insight, is so fundamentally the business of fiction that it's worth taking care with.

And by the way: don't break viewpoint in the middle of a scene. I just wanted to remind you, in case you forgot.

CHAPTER 4

"SHUT UP!" HE EXPLAINED— HANDLING EXPOSITION

AT THE BEGINNING OF YOUR STORY, you're going to have to decide how to convey necessary background facts. That's exposition.

Exposition involves breaking away from the ongoing action to give information—for a paragraph, or for a page or more. It's the author telling the reader something—telling, rather than showing.

As I explained earlier, telling is much less effective than showing. It follows that exposition is less dramatic and less vivid than a scene—generally, a *lot* less.

So, as with all major components of narrative, you'll need to recognize the nature of the problem and find effective, appropriate ways of compensating.

WHY EXPLAIN?

You may be asking, reasonably enough, if exposition is so dull, why not stick to scenes? Well, you can, if you want to and your story will allow it. A good many short stories are one single scene with no more than a phrase or two of exposition or description in any one place. Hemingway's stories are almost all sparse like that. Some novels, like Jack Shaefer's classic western *Shane*, can be all present-time, all surface, and yet be powerful in a stark kind of way.

But doing without exposition can be a problem too. Not all writers want to sound like Hemingway, and not all stories can be limited to immediate, direct action with no past, no context, no overview.

Scenes are, of their nature, close-focus. Having nothing but scenes would be like a movie all in close-up, with no establishing shots, no panning across the landscape to reveal eventual figures far away. That can feel pretty claustrophobic and nearsighted, after awhile.

Well-handled exposition gives perspective, dimension, and needed context that help events in the foreground make sense. Watching only scenes, in long or complex fiction, would be like trying to follow a baseball game through the wrong end of the binoculars. You'd have a lot of motion, all right—but the larger motions of the game would be extremely hard to follow.

In fiction, doing completely without explanations would mean you couldn't describe a person or place for more than a phrase or two. You couldn't skip over periods of time when nothing of importance is happening, not without a jarring break in the narrative. You couldn't take a confusing, close-focus series of events, draw back, and give the reader an overview of what it all means. You couldn't tell about any of the characters' background or previous experience.

Worst of all, maybe, you'd find it very hard to begin *in medias res*, in the middle of things—you couldn't pull back after the initial scene and say how things got that way. That would be a real handicap.

Even scenes, wonderful scenes, have their trade-offs, their problems that require compensation. Even high drama needs relief and context and overview. And that's the special job nothing can supply but the more distant, less immediate, more thoughtful kind of storytelling: exposition.

So in practice, fiction is a balance between scene and explanation—70%/30% or maybe even 80%/20%.

There may not be much explanation, but nothing else can do its work so economically or so well.

There also is nothing else that can kill a story quicker than explanation taking over, exposition badly handled.

Like viewpoint shifts, it needs to be treated with utmost respect, care, and narrative craft.

BURIED IN FOOTNOTES

I knew a writer who had nightmares about tons of exposition slithering down on her like a landslide. It can feel like that to a reader, too: smothering deluges of fact that prevent any motion at all. Ever read a textbook with lots of footnotes? Remember how you tended to skip or ignore the footnotes? Now, those of you who've read *Moby Dick*: how many of you actually *read* every word of the cetology chapters telling the folklore, anatomy, and habits of whales?

(Being a thorough-going nature nut, I personally enjoy the cetology chapters. Just like a nice National Geographic special. But I know a lot of folk who feel otherwise.)

Exposition is the curse of several of the popular genres, including science fiction, fantasy, and mystery. There are all those facts to be explained: maybe a whole new universe to be accounted for, the languages and customs of the Elven races, not to mention all those suspects and alibis! Westerns and historical fiction, necessarily built on a bedrock of research, are perhaps even more prone to this problem. If these facts, research, and outright invention aren't controlled and subordinated to the plot's needs, they can take over and literally bury a story in footnotes masquerading as narration.

WORLD-BUILDERS' DISEASE

For a writer, constructing the background material can be so much fun that it's mistaken for writing. Fantasy writers have a penchant for working up histories of imaginary empires that can run to hundreds of pages, full of maps and chronologies and genealogical trees a yard long. It's a common phenomenon: C. S. Lewis, in childhood, chronicled the doings of "Animal Land"; as adolescents, the Brontës produced long histories of an imaginary kingdom called "Angria." The whole of *The Silmirillion* and those long, long appendices are background information Tolkien wisely excluded from his huge trilogy, *The Lord of the Rings*—and certainly not for lack of space.

Similarly, science fiction writers can fall in love with their hardware and want to show it off, like a neighbor's interminable discussion of the gastric workings of his new car. George Lucas has commented that some sf movies are particularly guilty of this—their directors figure they've spent so much on a special effect that they use vital screen (storytelling) time giving a boring guided tour of some particularly elaborate model, relegating plot and character to the background shadows. Seen *Star Trek: the Movie*, with its seemingly interminable shots of the *Enterprise*? Writers can do precisely the same thing on paper.

Or sometimes sf writers can become so immersed in the sociology of the alien race they've invented that they offer glossaries translating native terms, folklore, sayings, and histories stretching back for millennia, in place of a story. Seen any of Ursula Le Guin's recent work, particularly *Always Coming Home*, which comes complete with an audio tape of folk songs?

Mystery writers can spend so much time working out alibis, with lists of suspects, timetables, maps with calculations on how long it would take to go by foot, bicycle, car or even helicopter to the scene of the crime, and the other logistics of detection, that they can't resist reusing these working notes in their stories. Dorothy L. Sayers' *The Five Red Herrings* is (among many excellent things) an exercise in timetable management; so is her *Have His Carcase*.

I call this phenomenon "World-Builders' disease." In its more extreme forms, it's narrative cancer: the unchecked and malignant growth of something that was harmless, even beneficial and necessary, in itself. In all genres, it involves becoming infatuated with the process of invention for its own sake. Exposition, essentially static and undramatic, isn't subordinated to plot and takes over. The story stops dead.

Pygmalion and Frankenstein

Every writer is Pygmalion, falling in love with his handiwork and wanting it to come alive. And sometimes, that love can be blind, as in the case of Pygmalion's dark counterpart, Dr. Frankenstein.

Writers blinded by the delights of concocting elaborate background material can forget that their primary job is to tell a story, not merely to invent.

Inventing is relatively easy—you take your expertise, whatever it may be, and project it on the universe. Tolkien, a medieval scholar and linguist, invented elaborate languages for dwarves, two races of elves, and several races of men. One of the human languages bore a striking resemblance to Old English, Tolkien's particular area of expertise. A plumber could invent a world full of plumbing, complete with detailed discussions of conduits, fittings, gravity-feed, and so on. A surgeon . . . no, that doesn't even bear thinking on.

As any bored spouse of a card player or a dedicated jogger knows, what's fun for one person to *do* isn't necessarily fun for another person to *watch*. Short of a tournament, chess just isn't a good spectator sport. Neither is working out exposition. Don't rent a stadium and expect crowds to flock in.

Don't assume your enjoyment in *doing* the invention is automatically going to mean the reader is going to enjoy the final product. Inventing is easy—it's storytelling that's hard. And it's storytelling the reader has a right to expect.

Give Your Reader a Piece of Your Mind—Not All of It

Rightly used, working background notes—what's sometimes called "doing your homework"—is the iceberg, and the story is the proverbial tip. The story is supported, sustained, given solidity and substance by a great mass of information the writer needs to know *but the reader doesn't—and shouldn't.*

The character charts some writing books advise you to make, calling for everything from a character's childhood nickname to his/her taste in furniture, can be useful. They can flesh out characters for you and let you start getting to know them preparatory to writing about them. Such charts are getting-ready exercises, not the race itself. A character in a story should be a character in action, not a walking mass of background data. Don't give in to the temptation to include in your story such working notes, however long, elaborate, and inventive they may be. The iceberg should stay out of sight to anchor the whole, not be on view to weight it down.

Keeping Exposition Under Control: Tolkien and Adams

To stop the story for long-winded explanations or descriptions is deadly, particularly at the beginning and most especially in the popular genres, where a strong, direct plot that moves along fairly briskly is an absolute necessity.

Follow Tolkien's example. He included the romance of Aragorn and Arwen Evenstar only as an appendix. That's because Tolkien was a storyteller to his very bones. He knew it didn't belong and would, however charming a tale in itself, have been a distraction, an impediment to the ongoing narrative.

Or follow Richard Adams' example. In *Watership Down*, the epic adventures of a group of rabbits setting out to found a new nation, Adams includes several tales of the rabbit folk hero, El-ahrairah. But he compensates. He gets his story well underway first and establishes his main characters before moving to the first tale. He makes sure each tale is brief, fairly simple (as folk tales generally are), and full of action, so it's dramatic rather than static. And he only departs from the main plot at a quiet moment, a lull between crises.

Moreover, each tale is connected by theme, mood, or actual content with the developments of the main plot. For instance, in one of the stories, El-ahrairah imitates the voice of a dog and, by guile, persuades a hostile animal to become his accomplice in stealing food. That's what gives the novel's protagonist, Hazel, the inspiration to lure a dog, as a dangerous but crucial ally, into a battle with invading rabbits, resolving the book's final crisis.

These folk tales are always kept carefully subordinate to the main plot and are never allowed to take over. Handling such an alternation is tricky in the extreme, but Adams brings it off successfully.

(You can see signs of impending world-builders' disease, though, in the fact that Adams includes, as an appendix, a glossary of rabbit language. A glossary, put afterward, when you've already struggled through the book without it, is always a dead give-away that the temptation to worse was there, even though successfully resisted.)

If you can't utterly put away your working notes, make them appendices—or wait until you're dead to issue them in book form, as is the case with *The Silmirillion*. Or keep the interruptions brief and full of action, and build in strong connections with the story proper to compensate.

Put your charts, glossaries, maps, and period newspapers in your sock drawer. Put them anywhere—except, undigested and unsubordinated, into your story.

The Story Comes First: Everything Else Is a Slow Second

The first, most important part of handling exposition is realizing that *it's going to need handling*. Once you're aware of that, you won't be as easily tempted to break off in the middle of an opening or a crisis to treat the reader to a completely unnecessary lecture on how the protagonist was frightened by a big dog in childhood or on the history of the building where the murder happened to take place.

Second, readers are only interested in explanation *after* their curiosity has already been aroused by something in need of explaining. In the beginning of a story, in particular, drop the people out of the plane and *then* say how they got there in the first place. Introduce your character, let him act and show himself and engage the reader's sympathies and curiosity. *Then* tell his background, if you need to.

In the middle of a story, exposition can serve as preparation for something that won't happen until later. But in its immediate context, it should *seem* called for by what's happened just before that point in the story. Otherwise, the exposition will just seem like a digression with no present relevance, or even like heavy-handed foreshadowing: nudging the reader and hinting obviously about what's coming, which none of the characters know—only the author. That's one form of authorial intrusion and something to be avoided, as I'll discuss further in a few minutes. Don't join the "Little did he/she know" school of writers. Make your hints fit in, inconspicuously, so they'll stay hints, not offensive authorial nudges.

Don't assume your responsibility as a writer automatically includes detailing every trauma, illness, or relationship a character had since birth. Neither does it require you to spell out every detail of sociology of the characters' social milieu or the history of the setting. Only important things, important to understand *this* story, *right now,* should be explained.

Important things. *Not everything!*

Be tough with exposition. Make each piece justify its inclusion—at all, and at that particular point of the story. It shouldn't be any longer than it has to be to do its essential work. Then get back to the plot again, as soon as possible.

PRESENTING EXPOSITION

So. You've decided what background material is really necessary in your story, and you've been careful to get your story up and running before breaking away for more than a paragraph or so to commit a stretch of exposition.

Now the question arises of how to present it.

Build It into the Scene

If you can, build it right into the scene. If it's important that the protagonist has been married before, invent some prop (a belated birthday card from ex-spouse? a final divorce decree in the mailbox?) or a bit of dialogue ("Mommy, is Daddy going to visit me this weekend?") that *shows* the fact without your having to say a word directly. Try to make each of your scenes multi-purpose: introducing or developing characters, moving the plot, and establishing immediately needed background, all at once.

Put It Between Scenes

If it's not just a fact or two but a mini-essay that's needed, it would be too confusing and cumbersome to try building it into the scene. In that case, the simplest way is just to tell it between scenes, with strong transitional connections to what goes before and what follows. Use objective narration: you're the all-seeing, all-knowing (but impersonal and invisible) narrator, and you just put in the information the reader is interested (you hope) in learning at that point in the story. That's the obvious choice for longer stretches of exposition, the one you'll probably use most often.

Let a Character Explain

The other choice is to have your characters give the necessary facts: one asks a question, and the other tells. Or one doesn't ask a question, but the other tells anyway. Or parts of the exposition can come out, a little at a time, in a discussion among several characters, maybe spread across several scenes. All these can work sometimes, if the exposition involved is brief and has other work to do at the same time, like revealing something about the characters involved. If, in other words, it serves a plot or characterization purpose as well as a strictly expositional one.

That has the advantage of keeping the story rolling while the exposition is going on. It's not as severe an interruption as it would have been if it were cast as objective narration, the disembodied author/narrator telling the reader directly.

But if the exposition is long or detailed, or if it's something the characters all know perfectly well, that form of presentation can be ridiculous and unconvincing. ("As you know, Harvey, our world was attacked by the eight-armed Arcturans seventy-six years ago and since then, we've all lived in these caves.") Don't ever put into a character's mouth anything that's strictly and obviously for the reader's consumption. Readers aren't fooled, and you've turned your characters into unconvincing puppets, dummies making silly speeches at each other.

Make It a Character's Interior Monologue

Finally, you can have the exposition as one character's reflections or thoughts—the fiction writer's version of a soliloquy. Your character can think about something, or recollect something, and thereby let the reader know what you want to convey. But be careful with this too. It stops the story; it's subject to the same abuses as exposition in dialogue; and if it's overdone, it can make your viewpoint character seem like a self-important pedant who just can't wait to lecture the reader.

There's a character like that in R. L. Stevenson's uncompleted story "The Wrong Box": a Victorian gentleman others flee because his favorite topics of conversation are things like how many times the word "whip" is mentioned in the Bible. In other words, he's a crashing and voluble bore. Don't let any of your characters turn into information-packed bores. You've undoubtedly met some in life. Why should anybody want to meet one in fiction—unless, like Stevenson's encyclopedic old Mr. Finsbury, they're also very funny?

THE DREADED AUTHORIAL FINSBURY

This brings me to a related matter: writers turning into Finsburys—lecturers droning on about some esoteric specialty—or into True Believers who see fiction primarily as a soapbox from which to promote some doctrine or belief, whether political, social, ethical, religious, ecological, or whatever.

Partly, this is related to the tradition of the omniscient author, which I discussed in the last chapter. Authorial intrusions—the story stopping dead while the author rambles on about whatever happens to interest him—used to be common-place, a hundred and a half years ago. (Need I again mention Melville's cetology chapters?)

Now, though, they're much disliked.

Although a story is of course nothing from first to last but an author's ideas anyway, we forget that, while we're reading. We treat the story as real, the characters as people we care and are concerned about. We imagine our way into it and don't want to be reminded it's an elaborate lie, a made thing, a puppet show in which some author is yanking the strings. To the degree that we're conscious of the puppeteer, that awareness keeps us from holding on to our conviction that words on a page can be worth our tears, our laughter, or our love.

Probably, any lecturing author is showing more than a few signs of world-builders' disease, too.

Don't become a Finsbury or a True Believer.

No matter how worthy your doctrine or how important or insightful your inside knowledge of the territorial battles of Sia-mese fighting fish, neither is storytelling. And storytelling is the primary business of fiction. Everything else comes second. It has to.

Does that mean I'm contending you shouldn't ever try to cast your convictions or your expert knowledge in the form of fiction? Of course not. Since the very beginnings of fiction, there have been wonderful, moving stories demonstrating some evil, social or personal. Think of Dickens and his attacks on Chan-cery, cruel schooling, the condition of the urban poor, and the "businesslike" barbarities exemplified by such characters as Scrooge, Mr. Dombey, and the elder Mr. Nickleby. Think of Hawthorne's *The Scarlet Letter* or Hardy's *Tess of the D'Urbervilles*. Think of Judith Rossner's *Looking for Mr. Goodbar* and Shirley Jackson's classic fable, "The Lottery." It's not hard to think of a dozen stories frankly embodying their authors' views on some social or moral issue.

Likewise, specialist information, carefully subordinated and sparingly doled out with a minimum of jargon, has given conviction, believability, and a unique slant to everything from stories about art-critic/detectives to fiction set on exotic plantations or in astronomical observatories, or featuring a protagonist who's a leper. Specialist detail comes under the heading, "If you've got it, flaunt it!" with just the recognition that flaunting doesn't involve letting it bury the story in footnotes.

If you want to include informational or polemical exposition, treat it as you would any problem element. Subordinate it, and compensate with all the narrative craft you've got.

Build it into the story, wherever the story will stand it.

Make it come alive so the reader can see it happening and mattering rather than being lectured by an author, either directly or by proxy, through some character.

Integrate it so thoroughly into the fabric of your story and your characters that it becomes part of their rightful structure and substance, bone and flesh, not just a series of labels, speeches, or footnotes.

KEEP OUT OF THE PLOT'S WAY

However you decide to handle exposition, of whatever kind, remember: the plot is paramount. Plot is the engine drawing everything else along. If you weigh it down with too much exposition, it's going to grind to a wheezing halt.

Limit exposition to the absolute essentials. Introduce it the least conspicuous, most natural-seeming way. Keep it as short as possible in any one place. Spread it across different scenes, if you can, according to where it's actually relevant and needed. And always make sure the present, immediate story is running strongly before breaking away from it for more than a paragraph or so. Leave your plot as unencumbered as possible. Let it move.

Judging the Balances in Popular Fiction

It's a question of proportion, of balance. The stronger, simpler, and more melodramatic your plot is, the more exposition it will stand (within reason) once the plot is rolling. If there's a murder on page one, readers will wait quite a few chapters, while the detective investigates this or that possibility and interviews suspects, until the next major event. That initial murder isn't forgotten. Once you've earned readers' confidence by an economical, powerful opening, readers will trust you not to let them down. They'll have faith that the buildup wasn't for nothing: something important is going to come of that first murder and there'll be more exciting dirty work afoot in the very near future.

The more complex, strange, and actionless your story is, the more you'll need to limit, digest, and subordinate your exposition, doling it out very sparingly indeed. That's particularly true in the most exposition-prone genres: science fiction, fantasy, mystery, and historical fiction of all sorts. If you're working in any of these forms, you're going to need to be particularly careful not to let unsubordinated exposition bog everything down.

With Literary Fiction, You Have to Make Your Best Judgment

Literary fiction is often complex, and isn't normally characterized by slam-bang zippy melodramatic plots. Readers of literary works are a more tolerant audience in some respects than are readers of popular fiction, though they're apt to be more exacting in others. They're remarkably patient with fairly long stretches where nothing much seems to be happening, provided they like the characters, or the writing style, or *something* about the story enough to keep reading.

There are folk like me who *like* the cetology chapters in *Moby Dick* and the long, bizarre ruminations in Mervyn Peake's *Gormenghast* trilogy, and folk who think of *War and Peace* or *Finnegans Wake* as a pleasant evening's entertainment. (All right, a weekend, then.) Plot isn't as crucial to such readers as it is to devotees of genre or popular fiction. As will be discussed in Chapter 11, literary fiction occasionally substitutes some other kind of strong motion or contrast for plot, so there may not even *be* a plot to subordinate the exposition to.

If, in your story, something else is substituting for plot—juxtaposition, contrast, collage, whatever—then keep *all other el-*

ements out of its way. If it serves plot's purpose as the bones, the dynamic engine of your story, then it's *that* which should be the basis of your choices of what to subordinate and what to leave clear, unencumbered, and dominant. If your story is built on a nested series of flashbacks, then character and plot come second. Exposition should be no more than a distant third in your narrative priorities.

Exposition is the thing in fiction most like thought, least like action. Decide how much thought your story will support, in proportion to its dominant element, and still remain compact, direct and readable. Then write it however it seems to need to be written.

Add Emotion and Stir Vigorously

Here's a tip based on a psychological quirk: we tend to remember best the information that comes to us surrounded by highly charged emotion. That's why so many people can remember precisely where they were and what they were doing when they first learned of the assassination of President Kennedy and how they spent their very first date.

Applied to exposition, this means that otherwise undigestible chunks of explanation will move faster, and be absorbed more easily, if they're put in a highly emotional context.

If you have some character really desperate for this information, the reader will tend to catch the infection and really want to know too. If you position the information in such a way that it has a strong and immediate emotional impact on somebody in the scene, it will become part of that scene's framework—hardly exposition at all. Or you can immerse your exposition in melodrama—whole situations which are emotionally charged—as I'll explain more in Chapter 7.

So now you know all the basic rules of effective exposition-cookery: move it fast, don't let it pile up too much in any one place, subordinate it to a strongly moving plot, and dip it in emotion whenever possible. Then, whenever you can, cut it out.

Become a Plot Surgeon

When you've got one whole first draft in hand, one of your first chores in beginning your second draft should be going back and cutting every scrap of exposition you find you can possibly do without.

There's an ancient joke that runs: *Want to lose ten pounds of ugly fat? Cut off your head.* Well, don't cut off your story's head. But in second draft, cut absolutely everything your story can do without—and that especially includes exposition.

CHAPTER 5

EARLY MIDDLES: NEW DIRECTIONS AND SUBPLOTS

REMEMBER AWHILE BACK, I WARNED YOU that every plot will try to go wrong after the first big scene?

It's true. Generally, it's because fiction fatigue has set in. You've been concentrating intensely, and now your beginning is complete, doing all the jobs that beginnings need to do.

Back off a day or two, catch your breath, before going any further.

But leave your beginning alone.

That's terrifically important. You'll be inclined to tinker with it, unsure that the hard choices of intuition and craft were the right ones, after all. And much of your second-guessing will be wrong. When you've just finished something is not the right time to revise it. You don't know where it all fits in yet—what it's leading up to. Your story doesn't have a real shape yet that can resist insecure tinkering.

Leave your beginning alone, at least until you have one whole first draft, in the case of a short story; or until you're past the middle, in a novel. Until then, you're not in a position to judge the fiction as one unified thing and make informed decisions about the individual sections.

If you have ideas for revision, fine. Jot them down, staple them to page one. Start a file of afterthoughts. But don't try to implement them—not yet. Your beginning may well benefit from revision; as I warned you earlier, you may even find you have to scrap it and start over. But not now.

I think more stories have collapsed from premature tinkering than from any other single cause.

Fiction fatigue: expect it, and don't let it ruin your story.

Let the beginning cool off enough to stand poking and prodding, before you go back to it. Instead, after a healthy rest mowing lawn or going to your job, start gearing up for the special tasks that middles involve.

AFTER THE OPENING, TAKE YOUR BEARINGS

I'll talk about short stories first because novels have to do exactly the same thing, only more so. (Novels have to do extra things, too, but don't worry about that now.)

If you followed my advice, you began *in medias res*. So there'll be things the reader will now be interested in knowing, to understand how matters came to be the way they were in the opening.

So you may decide to insert some exposition at this point or even a dramatized flashback, where past temporarily becomes present. These can do any of a variety of chores.

A New Perspective on Your People

You can broaden the reader's understanding of a character by giving a highly selective account of his past, distant or immediate. Emphasize just the two or three (or so) things which are going to be of significance in your story's present context. As I've said before: Important things—not everything.

Or you may follow the character as he goes about his present business, as Dickens does with Scrooge: trudging home through the holiday streets from his frigid office to his frigid house, starting to eat his wretched supper.

You can get into a full-blown character sketch, establishing some contrary facet of your protagonist that wasn't apparent in the opening. The huge, wilfully unattractive protagonist of Flannery O'Connor's "Good Country People," lumbering around on her artificial leg, is shown to be a highly intelligent, sardonic observer of her rapacious and hypocritical circle of rustic acquaintance.

Naming the Norm

If you're going to establish departure from a norm or a then/now contrast, it's a good time to lay the groundwork for it.

After its beginning, Katherine Anne Porter's *Noon Wine* shows the newly-hired and mysterious stranger at work in the fields and playing his cherished harmonica, at peace with himself and his surroundings—a peace that will be broken when the farmer discovers the hired man is on the run from a murder. This second section establishes a norm the story's later developments can be contrasted against.

Or the norm may be environmental—the character's society he or she is at odds with. In many of the stories in *Dubliners,* James Joyce follows that pattern: first giving a close focus on the protagonist, then showing the character's social world, demonstrating common attitudes and customs to present the protagonist in clearer social perspective. If your story has the main character in conflict with his immediate society and social norms, you may want to try this kind of opening-out too.

Switch Viewpoints?

The shortest fiction can seldom support more than one viewpoint. But now the first scene is over; if you're going to change viewpoints at all during your story, here's where you should do it for the first time to establish the pattern for the rest of the story. Thus your character sketch may center, instead, on the story's antagonist, profiling him or her in a way that shows why a collision course with the protagonist is inevitable.

Driving Right for the Cliff

Of course, you may plan a story that maintains tight focus to the end, with scarcely any exposition at all and perhaps just two characters. Many of Poe's short stories follow that pattern; I think of the narrator and doomed, foolish Fortunato, who provide the entire cast of "The Cask of Amontillado." And the plot is down the stairs and down the stairs, pausing only to collect wine and brandish the necessary mason's trowel as the narrator prepares to wall his victim up in the ancestral wine vaults to avenge a (perhaps) imagined insult.

That's the pattern in most genre short stories. The story flies like an arrow and hits the target at maximum speed.

If your story is going to have a direct, unencumbered narrative line with no digressions or shifts and virtually no exposition of any sort, then from the opening you'll continue the same scene or move right to another, with no interval at all.

The Janus-Faced Interval

Whether you're writing short or long fiction and whatever the section following the beginning is, it's got two chores: to open up the beginning by looking backward or simply around, adding context; and to look anxiously forward and lay the groundwork for what's to come. The Roman god Janus, the god of doorways for whom January is named, had two faces so he could look both ahead and behind. That's what you need to do, after a story's first beginnings. I'll talk about methods of doing that kind of necessary spadework in a minute. But this part of your story is where it starts in earnest.

GEARING UP FOR THE LONG HAUL

Now, the good news for the novelists out there: everything I've just been explaining applies to you too, but you've got more space to do it. You can devote a whole chapter or two to this second part, if you want. Probably there'll be scenes as well as straight exposition, to keep things rolling; but a strong effective beginning will win your readers. They're on your side now.

They've picked up the book. They know everything isn't going to be over in three or four pages. That's the way they want it, if they like novels. They'll stay with you now, unless you do something to lose them.

The looking-forward aspect of early middles is even more important for you, though, than for the short story writers. There's short-term plot and long-term plot, and both have to be running at once, either together or in alternation.

Stages in the Journey

Remember, *plot is a verb*. Something is happening, and going to happen. But there are stages to plot, and in long fiction there should always be some specific event in the not-too-distant future the reader can anticipate. The main or long-term plot ideally runs through the whole story from the beginning. It's what the opening centers on; it provides the final climax or confrontation.

In *Lord of the Flies*, the castaway boys' immediate problems are, in sequence: establishing order, lighting a fire, hunting a wild pig, exploring the island, and dealing with their dread of "the Beast" they believe is on top of the mountain. More problems follow. But each of these intermediate problems is a stage in the larger problem of staying alive, and civilized. The whole long-term problem is broken up into a series of actions, each of which has its crisis and resolution. For instance, the problem of gathering the castaway boys together is solved by the finding and blowing of the conch. The problem of making fire is solved by Piggy's glasses, concentrating the sun's rays. But the solution sets up a later problem, when the breakaway tribe led by Jack steals the glasses and deprives Ralph's group of fire and Piggy of sight/ vision (not precisely the same thing, in this book).

One problem or crisis builds to another, and another yet beyond. You need to have the main plot firmly in mind all along and be building toward the final crisis—in *Lord of the Flies*, the murderous pursuit of Ralph by painted, screaming savages driven by fear and superstition. You may not, at the early stages of the story, know precisely what that final crisis is going to be. That's all right. I'll offer some advice about endings in Chapter 10. Early in the story, just know that you should be building toward that ultimate crisis and that it should derive from the main plot as it was in the beginning, not from something weird and unexpected that turns up someplace along the way.

Setting Up Subplots

Often long fiction will have more than one plot. The subplot(s) may run just a while before coming to resolution, or may continue through almost the whole story, being tied up just before the story's end. Sometimes subplots center on the main plot's protagonist, and sometimes they focus on one of the subordinate characters.

Well handled, they can deepen the story's context, offer ways to mirror or contrast with the main action, and be used in pacing to offer foreground motion while the main plot is in a temporary lull. When the main plot is busy, they can generate suspense when the narrative splits off to follow the subplot for a while before rejoining the main action, generally with added momentum and impact when they again converge.

If you're going to have one or more subplots centering on the main characters, start the first one running right after the beginning. For instance, your protagonist, Fred, not only wants to avoid rescuing Ginger from the roof—he also wants to prevent anybody else from rescuing her. This involves sabotaging the walkie-talkies before they're issued, one per boat crew. Or Fred is in fact a concert violinist and is worried that his flood rescue efforts will mean he won't be able to get to his solo appearance in Detroit. And he's worried Ginger may not have taken his centuries-old Stradivarius to safety up onto the roof with her. He wants to rescue the Strad, but not Ginger. Conflict!

But if you're going to have a subplot centering on somebody other than the protagonist, don't treat it separately just yet. (Remember Tiffany, stuck in the tree?) Instead, introduce the subordinate characters central to the subplot so the reader can get to know them before the narrative line splits off to follow them.

Maybe a flashback to the last argument between Ginger and Fred, when Tiffany ran out shouting that she wanted to live with Grandma. Then, when main plot and subplot are running simultaneously, you can switch off to follow Tiffany all by herself. Maybe she got caught in the tree while trying to run away to Grandma's house forever. Maybe she's worried about Grandma, or having second thoughts about running away. Maybe Grandma's up in the tree with her.

Whatever, it's an independent (though closely related) subplot. Lay some groundwork and establish your main plot firmly before splitting off to follow another line of action.

Try a Braid

In long fiction, plots don't merely alternate with subplots: they're often woven together in something very like a braid. One strand loops around to the outside, out of sight, then warps in or under to briefly become the central point before warping off for another turn.

Once you have your initial situation running, with the major characters established and facing some crucial problem the reader can tell isn't going to go away, a braided plot won't just continue on. You'll bring in a new subject, one that has some new plot thread which you make clear but leave unresolved so that the reader can see that there are more developments to come.

You can braid that way two, three, even four times before you pick up strand A again and continue to new developments in that plot for a little while. Then C loops back, and B perhaps crosses over it to make a new pattern. Aha! Here comes D!

The stronger and clearer your individual plot threads are, the thicker the braid you can make. But a braid, like a chain, is only as strong as its weakest element. If one plot thread—especially your main one—is fragile, delicate, subtle, even confusing, be careful not to warp it more than it will stand or strangle it with subplots pulling this way and that. A braided plot can have so many twists and turns that it becomes something like a lump of fouled fishing line no sane reader's going to try to disentangle.

Be sure there's always a strong central narrative thread the reader can follow in spite of diversions and interruptions.

If your central plot is built on hints and slow unfoldings rather than on a series of clear and decisive developments, cut the number of subplots way back, maybe even to none. Conversely, if your main plot is as direct as a falling piano (something like boy meets girl, boy loses girl, boy and girl find one another), then braiding can broaden your story's scope and add narrative interest to an otherwise thin, straight-line, and predictable tale.

Multiple-strand plotting can yield a good solid braid if you watch out for dangling loose ends and keep tension strong at all times. Try a two or three strand braid, to start with. Then, as you learn the feel, you can expand to as many strands as you have pages and plot enough to spin out of your imagination.

Don't Forget to Knot as You Go

Remember what I said about alternating viewpoint: that the story will try to split in two? That's even more true when it comes to subplots. Knot the different strands of your narrative together from time to time. Build in all the connections and convergences you can. Show events in the main plot affecting what's happening in the subplot, and the other way round. Have characters overlap, figuring in both main plot and subplot, although perhaps more important in one than the other. For instance, in *Wuthering Heights*, Heathcliff is one of the main protagonists of the plot as a whole; but in the subplot detailing the successive romances between young Cathy and her two cousins (one of them Heathcliff's son), Heathcliff becomes a background figure, like a thunderstorm grumbling in the distance.

Build in connections of mood, event, props, setting, and narrative pattern, as I'll discuss more in Chapter 8.

Finally, remember that like main plots, subplots need developments, crisis, big scenes, and resolution. Even if a subplot is only going to run for thirty pages or so before coming to final crisis, it deserves the same care, in miniature, as does your main plot. Don't neglect it. Refer to it from time to time. If possible, make the subplot's crisis coincide with, and be directly involved in, an important crisis in the main plot. Converging plot lines will add to the whole scene's impact and meaning.

For instance, you shouldn't kill off your protagonist in mid-plot; but you can kill off an important subordinate character who's been the center of a subplot. The implied threat to the protagonist will be intensified. And if you really like the subordinate character, you can write him or her a wonderful death scene and maybe throw a spectacular funeral.

Parallel Plotlines

Sometimes judging which is main plot and which is subplot is about like tossing a coin. Both seem about equal. Perhaps the most familiar example of that would be the contrasting adventures of Han Solo, Princess Leia, and Chewbacca, on the one hand, and of Luke and Yoda, on the other, in George Lucas' movie *The Empire Strikes Back*, the second segment of his *Star Wars* trilogy.

All the characters are initially established together, at the secret rebel base tunneled into the ice. Since the ending of the story will involve Luke's rash and unsuccessful attempt to rescue Han from Darth Vader, a similar situation is set up in the beginning, where Han rescues Luke from being frozen to death. By no coincidence, Han's peril from Vader also involves his being frozen, although in something called "carbonite," not ordinary ice. The opening crisis mirrors the ending.

Likewise, Luke's initial resourcefulness in killing a snow monster and in singlehandedly destroying a huge, walking tank mirrors his lone battle with Vader at the movie's end. Since in the middle Luke is shown failing, blundering, whining, and not doing too much exciting, the action-filled beginning and end prevent him from looking like an incompetent wimp.

The beginning provides contrast and context for the middle. It's also strongly tied to the ending, to help hold the middle together.

The middle needs all the tying it can get, because in the middle, two plots split apart to follow different protagonists. The narrative line cuts back and forth between them. The part of the story focused on Han & Co. is a fairly straight chase/adventure with a romance thrown in. Luke's plot, more subtle and thoughtful, involves his education by Yoda in the nature and use of the Force—a more interior plot with hardly any action at all and certainly no romance.

I've found it interesting which among my friends prefers the Han plot and which the Luke plot, in this movie. Whichever you like better, notice the differences in subject, pacing, and tone in the divergent sections. Pains were taken to balance the comparatively less dramatic account of Luke's education with the lasers-blasting escaping and hiding and capture involved with Han & Co. Each plot is the richer and stronger for being contrasted with the other.

And notice how connections were built in. Although Han & Co. are completely occupied with their own problems, Luke becomes aware of them through a vision. That awareness and feeling of connectedness is what prompts Luke to leave although his training hasn't been completed. So Luke's awareness is a bridge between the two plot lines. Another is the fact that Han & Co. are captured by Darth Vader primarily as bait, to bring the real target—Luke—into Vader's reach.

But there are even more obvious connections—events repeated in slightly different form in each plot line. For instance, both plots involve the sudden and unexpected appearance of Darth Vader. For Luke, Vader appears as a malignant vision of possibility and identification (the illusory Vader has Luke's face), laying the groundwork both for the later duel and for the revelation that Vader is Luke's father; for Han & Co., Vader appears as an even more malignant reality. Both plots involve journeys. Han & Co.'s journey is primarily across space, whereas Luke's is mainly one of interior growth and insight—to and through the dark spaces in his own soul, moving from self-doubt to confidence (maybe even overconfidence). Both protagonists meet old friends: Han encounters Lando, and Luke finds he's still under the not-quite-ghostly oversight of Obi-Wan Kenobi, the dead (?) Jedi master. Both plots involve a cave where things aren't quite what they seem. Han parks his souped-up space jalopy somewhere in the interior of a mammoth space worm which, open-mouthed, fills the cave—the cave is a monster in literal fact. In Luke's cave, he finds the dreadful shadows of his own interior made manifest: his own fear and hatred take form as the figure of Vader, the threatening monster.

In each case, what in the Han plot is external, a physical reality is, in the Luke plot, internal—a realization or a vision. Internal and external balance, connect.

Then, after this middle section, the plots converge again in Luke's attempt to rescue Han & Co. and his first face-to-face confrontation with Vader. Luke joins the Han plot.

Together, apart, together. But even during the separation, many connections and echoes keep the two plots strongly interconnected and related. And suspense is created as the narrative line shifts from the one to the other, typically at cliffhangers in the Han plot, so we're kept waiting to find out how things are going back in the asteroid belt or in the Cloud City.

This is a story that could easily have fragmented; but it's held together by strong and effective narrative rivets so that the whole works as one single connected action.

Even though I assume most of you aren't planning to write space-opera melodrama, the structure of this story serves as a valuable demonstration of the basic techniques of handling parallel and equal plot lines. Reviewing it on videotape, if you have a VCR, can reveal still other connective devices, echoes, mirrors, and pacing techniques you'll find useful no matter what kind of fiction you're interested in.

Though there are all kinds of fiction there's only one craft. What works for one story will likely work for another, and all good works of craft repay thoughtful study.

If you're contemplating a divided plot structure, spend this after-beginning section strongly establishing your characters and their relationships, and creating scenes and events you can echo later on, to be a solid basis for the coming split.

Because after this, things are going to get *really* interesting. In just a few paragraphs or pages, you'll be looking toward your first major crisis, your first Big Scene, where the plot is really going to thicken and knot and spit sparks in all directions.

CHAPTER 6

BUILDING THE BIG SCENES: SET- PIECES

THE JOB OF A MIDDLE is to build toward and deliver crisis. That's true whether you're working in long-form or short-form fiction.

And since scenes are the foundation of fiction, the foundation of plots are special scenes, big scenes. They're generally called set-pieces—I'm not sure why. Maybe it's because they need setting up to be effective.

SLOWLY IT TURNS, STEP BY STEP

Stories, especially long fiction, need to be divided into stages, intermediate short-term plots, each with its own build-up, crisis, and resolution. Before Frodo and Sam can reach Mount Doom to destroy the terrible Ring, they have to reach Rivendell and Lorien and pass through Shelob's lair. Before Sam Spade can find out who killed his partner, he has to disarm Joel Cairo and the gunsel, dodge his partner's jealous wife and the police she sets on him, and find out who the Fat Man is and what this black bird is that everybody seems so interested in.

Even if your story is a journey through time or one of realization and revelation, rather than one across distance, it's still a journey. There need to be destinations, memorable landmarks, and even rest stops, several of them, before it reaches the final goal.

Set-Pieces

These intermediate moments of climax and partial, temporary resolution are what set-pieces are designed to provide. A set-piece is a big scene the reader can see coming and can look forward to awhile, either in fear or in hope, before it's reached. The duel between Luke and Darth Vader is a set-piece. The burning of Atlanta, in *Gone With the Wind*, is another. In *Lord of the Flies*, Simon's journey up the mountain to see what's *really* up there, monster or not, is a set-piece, as is his return into the middle of the hysterical tribal dance by which the boys are trying to drive out fear. Simon is mistaken for the Beast and killed. We could see it coming, even though Simon didn't. We weren't sure—we hoped for the best, but suspected the worst.

Seeing a scene like that coming, watching it build to crisis, is one of the major ways of creating tension, drama, and suspense in a story.

The earliest set-pieces will be the hardest, because they'll still have expositional chores to do—developing the characters, demonstrating the nature of the conflict, establishing the setting, and so on. They'll also have the briefest preparation. The later ones can be more streamlined and direct. You'll have your little world set up fairly completely in all its complexities by then; the reader will already know your characters and appreciate what's at stake, and you'll have had time to lay your groundwork to build toward the set-piece that's coming.

Being more direct, and carrying the whole foregoing story's momentum behind them, these later set-pieces will gain in impact and drama. You and your story will be up to speed then: in third gear, and rolling fast. Later set-pieces will be easier to write.

Remember that and take heart: after the beginning, and after the sections immediately following, it gets easier. The story itself will be on your side, helping you to create and move.

If you choose your set-pieces well, build up to them so that the reader can see what's coming, *and deliver on them*, your story will be good reading from beginning to end.

Delivering on Set-Pieces

I emphasize *delivering* because far too many beginning writers get terminally shy about their set-pieces. They dodge away into talk, or skip the scene and maybe refer afterward to what happened. They'll do every blessed thing except actually *write the scene*.

I don't know how or why this kind of fundamental narrative timidity originates (although, rereading my own early stories, I see that I suffered from a touch of it too, here and there). I only know I've seen quite a lot of it, mostly in unpublished work.

Maybe intuitively such beginners realize that a set-piece is the third most important part of any story, after the opening and the ending. Maybe they realize their story is going to stand or fall by the scene coming up, and they just can't face the responsibility of writing it and being judged by it. They're afraid to commit themselves and go for broke. So instead, they skitter off into exposition or summary, and the story sags.

Face up to set-pieces. Make up your mind to write them, even if—*especially if*—you're afraid to. If you see that things in your story are heading toward a blowup between Ginger and Fred pretty soon, show the tension building up, show the hurt feelings accumulating, and then blow everything sky-high. Make their blowup happen at a party, on a train station, or someplace where neither can get away until they've both had their hurtful say. Use the setting to complement or contrast strongly with the action. Write the battle as though it were a new beginning, with that much clarity and intensity.

Write the scene.

Notice and polish every legitimate, intrinsic bit of drama inherent in the scene until it absolutely glitters. Embody that drama in action—things done, things said, in a *scene* happening right before the reader's eyes.

Not All the Scenery Has to Show Tooth Marks, Though

When I say "write the scene," I don't mean overwrite it. If what you're writing is a domestic quarrel, don't throw in a burglar or attacking commandos or the kitchen sink just because it would make the scene dramatic. That sort of overkill will only push the scene over the edge into farce.

What I mean is that, whatever your set-piece is, you should bring out all its facets and polish it like a jewel. Make it the best domestic quarrel anybody ever wrote, one the neighbors would buy tickets to watch, not a garbled, hodgepodge screaming match with tanks bursting in.

Write the scene so that something has completely happened, every bit. More will undoubtedly come of it later on, but this one scene shines. Frodo really does resist the Dark Riders at the ford, at least long enough for wizardly help to arrive. Simon really does see, clear and plain, what horrible, pitiable thing actually is on top of the mountain.

Setting Up What's to Come

Now, after the beginning that set up the major narrative and structural patterns, and after the opening section where your plot really got rolling, you should start imagining where, in the short run, your story is going. What major event, several pages or chapters ahead, is going to happen? Start imagining it. Who will be there? What's going to lead to it? And what's going to happen? What will you need to establish beforehand, so that set-piece can have its full weight and impact? How can you go about laying that necessary groundwork now, where you are in the story?

As I've said before, stories—especially live, convincing stories—will change under your hands. That's the reason I've never been persuaded of the usefulness of outlines. By other writers' experience and my own, I judge that you generally won't know how a story's going to go until you get close to the place where something is just about to happen. It will take its own shape and tell you how it wants to go, if you listen and watch attentively for the ways it's telling you.

My advice is that you should always know what your next set-piece is going to be. You should be laying the groundwork for it right up to the time it happens. You should start that groundwork either from the story's beginning, or lay down the first seeds back before the previous set-piece, to mature and bloom later. And you should be thinking of how that set-piece relates to your main story and making sure it won't seem grafted on, invented on the spot, but is a natural outcome of everything that's gone before.

It can't be just any scene, either. You'll have only about a dozen set-pieces in a whole long novel; in a more compact book, there will probably be more like six. In short fiction, perhaps three: beginning, middle, and end. Or, in the tightest and most focused of short stories, maybe only one. These set-pieces are going to be your story's high points; the scenes a reader will remember when the build-up, transition, and explanation have all been forgotten; the scenes where your plot rises to crisis.

So choose them well. As much as possible, let your story generate them. Let them arise out of who your people are, what problems they're facing, what they're trying to do—the story's central conflict. After they're in place, they'll seem inevitable, as if nothing else could possibly have happened. But you have to make them up: not quite out of nothing, but out of the body and bone of your story as it takes shape under your hands.

Things Get Blacker and Blacker

In long fiction, scene builds on scene, set-piece on set-piece. The impact isn't isolated, but cumulative. It becomes a story's momentum, its pace (about which, more in Chapter 9.)

Very often, several or even all of the intermediate crises will be disasters, with matters apparently much worse than before. The protagonist will be defeated, though not quite utterly. This increases tension and suspense, acting as build-up for the final crisis. But each of the intermediate crises also should open a new door, present a fresh opportunity, offer a revelation as to the real nature of the problem the protagonist faces. In Charlotte Brontë's *Jane Eyre*, the attic conceals brooding Rochester's first wife, and every crisis in Jane's romance brings her nearer that crucial discovery. Daphne du Maurier's *Rebecca* is also founded on a fundamental lie—that Rebecca, Maxim's dead first wife, was a paragon whom Maxim loved profoundly and now mourns continually. Every major crisis the young protagonist faces unravels part of that lie to disclose the truth: that Rebecca was an unfaithful and unfeeling wife whom Maxim came to hate deeply, perhaps to the point of murder.

To the degree that your plot is a mystery, your set-pieces should provide, not only crisis, but unfolding revelation of a central truth concealed at the story's beginning and not completely demonstrated until the final crisis.

But it's not just mysteries which set-pieces can reveal. Remember, plot involves actions with meaningful consequences. Such consequences evolve, one step at a time. Each set-piece (after the first) should be set in motion, at least in part, by what happened in the previous one. This present scene should dramatize and arise from the effects created by what's gone before, and in turn have effects played out in the story thereafter. Cause sparks effect, which in turn becomes cause, right up to your story's end.

Using the existing story as a step from which to find and reach the next level of tension and crisis is what creates unity in long fiction: the feeling that all the parts are necessary to the whole and are meaningfully connected, each with the others.

Outlining from Inside

When you've written your set-piece, you should be looking ahead to the end, to see if you can see its shape any more clearly from this vantage point than you could before. And if you can, make adjustments to make this scene lead more clearly, more precisely, toward the last cliff, with fewer possible turnings-away, so that the story, crisis by crisis, narrows down to a point that seems inevitable when it comes.

I call it outlining from inside. Blocking out the story, one set-piece step at a time, from inside it, taking due account of what it seems so far to be trying to become. That much outlining, I believe, every writer needs if his story is not to appear a funhouse, a random series of events sprung on the reader for no particular reason, gone too fast to have impact, leading from nothing to nothing. You need some kind of an outline, some idea of where you're going and how, if you're going to keep your story out of the funhouse which, in fiction, is no fun at all.

Look ahead at least to your next major scene and get ready for it. Then deliver.

But Don't Hint It to Death

In your build-up, though, take care not to try to write the set-piece before it's ready, before it's had a chance to simmer properly. Establish that it's coming, and maybe hint at the basic nature of the confrontation. You've established your characters, so the reader has some idea how each will react in crisis. But don't give away the exact crisis, or the outcome. Leave that for the scene itself. Grant the reader not only the enjoyments of looking forward but the enjoyments of discovery, scene by scene, as well. Write your set-pieces boldly and thoroughly, but keep some of your cards hidden right up to the end.

Or Serve It With a Twist

If the outcome, or the crisis itself, seems too predictable, like the traditional western gunfight, you can throw in maybe one surprise element—not attacking guerrillas, but something you've carefully refrained from hinting about. If you've set the stage for a duel, deliver a duel, all right—but fought with dynamite instead of guns. If your build-up has promised an explosion at a bank, deliver an explosion—but one that not only opens the safe but sets fire to the thieves' getaway car.

Never fail to deliver what, implicitly or explicitly, you've promised your reader. But don't assume you have to serve it up in the same, predictable old dish, either.

Your sudden twist mustn't change the basis of the confrontation itself, like guerrillas in the middle of a domestic argument (unless, of course, you're writing surrealistic farce, in which case all bets are off, anyway: even twittering nine-armed Martians are legal, then, if they work). The mood and meaning should be the same, regardless of the twist. Don't make the scene anticlimactic, like a duel that's fought with wet spaghetti or water balloons, or a

ball where friends try to keep the feuding male and female protagonists apart—and succeed, so nothing happens after all.

Play with Murphy's Law. Try to think of what, within that
fundamental situation, could go surprisingly wrong, yet seem
believable and reasonable, within that context, when it happens.

For instance, on the mountain, Simon finds, not a monster,
but a dead pilot. But since Jack's tribe is in the process of turning
into warriors, and since the irrevocable step in that transformation is their killing of Simon, a dead soldier isn't a neutral thing
either. It's the essential savagery and warlike inclinations of humanity that's the Beast in the book. So it's a real Beast, *the* real
and only beast, which Simon discovers. It's just not the sort of
beast either Simon or the reader had expected.

The scene throws in a twist, but it works. It delivers true
monsterdom, in the book's special context, and monstrous
things come of the discovery. It works better than it would have
if Simon found nothing, or Godzilla. And part of its being better
is the surprise twist that makes more sense than finding either
nothing or a trampling reptile, because it's appropriate to its
context. We couldn't have predicted it, but it fits. It works. It's a
masterly twist—one of many in the book. There's another at the
end. And, no, I'm not going to tell you how it all comes out.

Read *Lord of the Flies*, if you haven't already. It's not cheery,
but you'll learn a lot about laying evidence, build-up, and delivering set-pieces from it. Also, if it's any inducement, it's short. . . .

LAYING THE GROUNDWORK

There are ways to prepare for an upcoming set-piece. Some of
them are obvious, some less so.

One obvious thing you need to do is simply naming the ap-
proaching event—the visit of the wealthy but irascible grandfa-
ther, the trip to the zoo, the battle at the river, the big dance or
exclusive party your protagonist yearns to be invited to. It would
seem just common sense to mention the event before it happens
and indicate, through characters' words and attitudes, why it's
likely to be climactic, but I'm always surprised how many writers

neglect this basic chore.

Maybe they figure if they spring their set-piece on the reader without preparing the ground, it'll be even more of a surprise. And it is—but not a good one. Without anticipation, a sudden crisis has all the drama of slipping on the ice and thumping your tailbone. There's no suspense, no anticipation—just the jolt, and it's over. Big deal. At least half the fun of any holiday is the looking forward. Apply that to your fiction, and prepare for your big scenes.

These no-build-up folk are the opposite of those I mentioned earlier: the ones who enjoy the hinting and the looking forward, but hate arriving, whose idea of effective surprise is that, after considerable preparation, *nothing* happens. Wow. Surprise. I trust you won't be tempted to join that coy and anticlimactic crew. You may have heard the saying, "It's better to travel hopefully than to arrive." Maybe so. But in fiction, you'd better do both or take up another trade, like fan dancing. There's only just so much hopeful traveling you can expect readers to do before they give up in annoyance and disappointment. After a strong beginning, you'll have some credit to draw on, but there are limits.

Use a Preview Scene

Another way to lay groundwork is to have a small preview scene where some form of the actual events of the coming set-piece are set up—a small duel or clash anticipating the big duel or clash. There's an instance of this in *The Empire Strikes Back*, which I discussed in the previous chapter: Luke has a laser-sword fight with an apparition of Darth Vader conjured in an evil cave (a fight Luke loses *because* he wins). Those few seconds are setup for the actual duel enacted in several distinct stages near the movie's conclusion. In that later duel, Luke loses but escapes defeat by casting himself into the unknown rather than allow himself to despair and surrender—a reverse mirror of the earlier fight where victory paradoxically meant defeat. Here, defeat leads to Luke's coming to terms with the truth, that Vader's his father: the pivotal insight which powers the trilogy's eventual and climactic reconciliation between them in *Return of the Jedi*.

If your set-piece is going to hinge on the fact that your protagonist has lost his glasses, show them being lost (and eventually found) a time or two beforehand. It will provide foreshadowing as well as make the important loss of the glasses, in the set-piece, entirely believable and convincing.

Use Contrasts and Make Things Get Much Worse or Much Better

Your set-piece will have the most impact if you lead up to it with scenes of varied length, but all brisk and relatively short. Then, when your set-piece arrives, your reader will be ready to settle down to something more substantial and intense.

If your set-piece is going to be a grim disaster, you have a choice—your lead-in scenes can be cheery, hopeful, or peaceful (suspicious readers will immediately start suspecting the worst) or else more and more troubled and disturbing. Then the scene will need to be not merely the confirmation of the characters' worst fears, but beyond anything they'd even imagined. (Merely confirming suspicions has little drama; finding out things are even worse than you'd thought leaves whole new vistas of unpleasantness to explore.)

But if your big scene is going to turn out wonderful and happy, the lead-in should probably be as black as possible. Cheer followed by more cheer, cute upon cute, can make even the nondiabetic among us wince. A touch of sour gives tang and helps ward off banality. Unrelieved sweetness, thoroughgoing uplift, becomes stronger and more persuasive by the addition of a dash of bitters, at least in anticipation, though your set-piece may open all sunny and go on to become positively idyllic and full of implicit happily-ever-afters.

Make Room for the Aftermath

How you lead your narrative out of a set-piece is just as important as how you lead it in.

The outcome of the set-piece has to *matter*, and needs to

have narrative and emotional space to matter in. After the big scene, the story should be changed and the characters meaningfully affected by what's happened. If everything goes on as before, the set-piece will seem much fuss and bother about nothing—empty, irrelevant, and finally disappointing, no matter how well written and dramatic in itself. It should not only arise from the story that goes before, but be a determining factor in the story that comes afterward.

Crises are sometimes called turning points. Make sure that, after a set-piece, the story does turn—into something even more absorbing and important. With each round, all bets are raised and more is at stake and at risk. By the story's end, everything of importance to the protagonist, in that particular context, should be at hazard, win or lose.

A Matter of Life and Death

In fiction for the widest readership, what's at stake will probably be life, love, or both, in the most literal and direct way. Somebody, or somebody's lover, could get killed. In less melodramatic fiction, the stakes may be self-respect, reconciliation, being true to oneself or to an ideal or a relationship. But these more subtle, interior stakes must in fact be just as high as those in stories where the protagonist faces purely physical and external threats.

The death of the self is also death, though the body may live on. An interior death is still a death to be feared and fought with all one's energy and wit. So is the death of the heart—the capacity to feel, as distinct from the threatened loss of a relationship or of a particular lover. The risk of becoming what one hates, committing the one unforgivable act, speaking the lie (or the truth) that can never be unsaid, are dangers perhaps more terrible than that of facing a loaded gun.

Whatever the actual terms of the risk, it should finally always become and be a matter of life and death—however life and death have been defined in this particular context, your own unique world. And the risk should escalate and intensify from the opening crisis right up to the end. With the whole weight of the book's context, the characters' development, and the build-ing momentum of the crises along the way to give it force and meaning, what seemed perhaps a minor threat or a small per-sonal desire at the beginning should, by story's end, be felt by the reader to be as profound as a clash of suns, in which all light will either fail or blaze triumphant.

Where everything's on the line, and that line keeps getting nearer the edge—that's a set-piece.

CHAPTER 7

HARNESSING MELODRAMA

MENTION MELODRAMA AND ALL IT CONJURES UP for some people is a wide-eyed heroine being tied to the train tracks by a moustache-twirling villain. But that's not it. Not by half.

If drama releases the electricity implicit in small events, melodrama calls down lightning.

Melodrama is the equivalent of a blinding flash accompanied by a loud noise. It can be a bony hand creeping from behind a curtain, a grand passion, someone teetering on a high ledge, or any of a thousand vivid situations and characters. Their meaning is right out in the open; they seem special, unusual, exciting. Such events speak directly to our imaginations and emotions.

Some people seem larger than life. Who and what they are is recognized at once. It's similar to the way a good caricature of a President or a celebrity can be more easily identified than an ordinary snapshot: a caricature draws in bold lines those features most associated with that person and downplays the unimportant ones. Some fictional characters seem larger than life: strong, interesting, dramatic. They too speak directly to our imaginations and emotions.

Melodrama is a technique of revealing reality by concentrating on the ends of the spectrum rather than the middle, the remarkable rather than the ordinary.

Events and individuals whose appeal and significance speak directly in this way, that don't need explaining, can immediately involve readers and arouse their sympathies. Using them in fiction can lead to forceful plots relatively unencumbered by exposition and peopled by vivid, colorful characters. For that reason, melodrama is the foundation of popular (genre) fiction, aimed at the broadest possible range of readers and intended primarily (but not solely) for entertainment.

Melodrama is also used, selectively and often with even greater impact, in literary fiction, which aims at a narrower readership and is intended primarily to present the author's view of the world/life/people. Because it's heightened, exaggerated reality, melodrama lends itself easily to symbolism, allegory, and surrealism, a different but related kind of exaggeration whereby the meanings implicit in objects, people, or events become more luminous and accessible than meanings normally are in the chaotic muddle of our everyday world. Sometimes visionary, heightened reality is the most real of all, because all the transitory, trivial details have been stripped away to reveal the fundamental essence of things.

The Power and Problems of Melodrama

Because melodrama ignores the ordinary to concentrate on the unusual and unlikely, it often creates a credibility problem. Because it chooses the heart over the head, the snap reaction over thoughtful consideration, emotion can go over the edge into sentimentality, tear-jerking, thrills or scares for their own sake, as empty of meaning as a whoopie cushion. Melodrama can therefore seem *or be* sensation-mongering, appealing to the lowest common denominator and our least intelligent responses; so it also has a respectability problem. But carefully managed, it has power.

At the best, it's as fundamental and useful as salt, heightening and bringing out the flavor of whatever it's added to; at the worst, it takes over and drowns all lesser seasonings and renders the dish uneatable. Such built-in power isn't something any writer can afford to dismiss or ignore without risking blandness. But it's not something to toss in by the handful, either.

Like myth, legend, and fairy tale, melodrama is a part of our common emotional and cultural language. Judiciously used, it can create instant rapport between writer and reader. It can be casting an effective spell—or it can be a curse, a pitch as blatant, annoying, and obvious as somebody stridently hawking used cars on late-night tv. It's a question of degree, and of craft.

Whether a given melodramatic event or character is effective or becomes a kind of emotional and literary cliché, trivializing the story in which it appears, is just a matter of how it's handled, set up, shown.

If your story is founded on melodrama—the death of a child, first love, God running a society of secret agents (Chesterton, *The Man Who Was Thursday*), a vampire opening red eyes, a maniac stalking and slaughtering teenagers—it will need to be handled with special care if it's to avoid being or seeming clichéd, overdone, or outright silly and weird.

TAMING WILD MELODRAMA

Curses are melodramatic—the ancient kind, especially in mysterious symbols on parchment, especially involving mummies. Especially curses that work. (Boasts Shakespeare's pompous Glendower, "I can call spirits from the vasty deep," to which Hotspur retorts sardonically, "Why, so can I, or so can any man; but will they come when you do call to them?")

So how can you have something like, say, a real working curse, something that actually *comes*, in your story and make the reader want to believe in it while the story lasts?

How can you encourage what literary critics have called "the willing suspension of disbelief" when your story is founded on something intrinsically unlikely, strikingly unusual, or even impossible?

Melodrama, what I'm going to call "the curse" as a kind of shorthand for discussion, can be any of a variety of events, horrible or wonderful: love, death, or both together. It can be the supernatural, the exotic, the strange, the highly improbable coincidence. It can be a monstrous or magical character, divorced from the usual range of human experience or capabilities.

Melodrama is extremes of any kind, things intended to rouse strong emotions and invoke implicit shared attitudes. Like Jacob wrestling with the angel, you can't let go of such powerful material until you've come to terms with it, turning the curse into a blessing.

Taking the Curse off the Curse

There are straightforward ways of setting your curse in the middle of solidly credible things and declaring it right from the beginning. There are other methods of misdirecting attention so that the curse has already happened and been accepted before the reader has a chance to holler, "Hey, now, wait a minute!"

I'll start with the front-loading ways first—putting the unusual right up front and making it part of the story's fundamental reality.

1. Show that it works, right away. Have your curse actually operating (or your vampire stalking, your magician performing prodigies, or whatever) right on page 1, so the reader knows that in this story, one of the rules is going to be that your particular curse works. Show it, don't tell it.

Star Wars starts out with a backdrop of stars and two spaceships blasting colored rays at another. Anne Rice's *Interview with the Vampire* starts out with a vampire talking into a tape recorder. Either way, you know pretty clearly what you're in for from the beginning. Each story demonstrates its central premise: modern vampires, or shoot-'em-up spaceflight. What you see is what you get.

If your story will be playing by rules other writers have used before—that vampires exist, that faster-than-light travel is possible—this may be the best way. Introduce your premise with as little fuss as possible and get on with your story, what you're going to be doing within that accepted convention.

If you're embarking on thoroughgoing surrealism, then make *that* clear from the outset. The unfortunate protagonist of Kafka's *Metamorphosis* doesn't turn into an insect halfway through but in the very first sentence. State the premise, make the rules of your fiction clear, and go on from there.

2. Show that the curse has worked in the recent past. Sometimes this way is better, particularly if you're working with an unusual premise that will be entirely new to your readers and that they'll therefore be more resistant to than a familiar one. That way, your curse becomes, not a possibility, but an accomplished fact.

We know there's no arguing with the past: it's over. That psychological quirk, our willingness to accept something that happened in the past more readily than something claimed in the present, can work for you.

This can include having your curse (or unusual character or event) talked about before he/she/it actually appears, to prepare the ground. That's the way Melville sets up Ahab.

Or you can have a past event for which no satisfactory explanation has ever been found. The story then demonstrates the cause in the present, which also explains the past, retroactively. The real and undoubted past event anchors and renders credible the present investigations, revelations, and developments.

You can also tie in the *in medias res* advice I gave earlier, in this regard—showing curse #2 threatening first, then dropping back to let the reader know about curse #1 (or the fact that three teenagers have already been found mysteriously hickory-smoked to death or whatever your improbable premise may be).

3. Establish a reasonable character, and have him take the curse seriously. Don't have anybody doubting it, at least not for long. As readers, we're used to fictional conventions. We'll accept that in one story there's a secret door to elfland, and in another, killer tomatoes are thumping toward New York. It doesn't really do any good, anymore, to have some stooge still claiming on p. 183, "It can't be: another head growing out of her WHAT?"

The reader gets annoyed at such a character, who's still resisting what the reader has already accepted as a basic premise. A resident Doubting Thomas doesn't defuse incredulity, as he once served to do in earlier fiction for a more literal-minded age; he just looks like a dolt.

Instead, have your whole cast of characters either ignorant of the curse, or worried/hopeful about it—just the one, or the other. Once the reader has accepted your premise, anybody who stubbornly refuses to do likewise is obviously a jerk (and you might want to use that fact to undercut a character at some point). Show that in your story, ordinary, reasonable people—not just those privy to the Secret Knowledge of the Ancients, like Dr. Van Helsing—take your premise very seriously indeed.

4. Surround your curse with tangible everyday objects and activities, described in detail. Paraphrasing the trenchant observation of a former Dr. Who, the Yeti (Abominable Snowman) you surprise in your suburban bathroom is a lot scarier than the one encountered on a glacier in exotic Tibet.

Realistic details make for realism. Alfred Hitchcock knew this, and made ordinary things the springboards for horrifying and unlikely occurrences: remember the shower scene in *Psycho*? Remember the birds roosting patiently (and in ever-increasing numbers) on the jungle gym, waiting for school to let out?

Things can get more and more bizarre as your story progresses, but if you anchor your improbability solidly in the everyday to begin with (nice urban professional couple—husband a little moody, wife pregnant: Ira Levin, *Rosemary's Baby*), the reader will accept it.

If you're going to have, as a character, the eight-armed ambassador from the Wobbly Worlds, don't introduce him/her/it doing something alien and incomprehensible. Open the story with him/her/it swearing at a cabdriver in midtown Manhattan or searching myriad pockets for change of a ten. Or have the alien doing something plain and simple, like watching the sunrise or playing a flute. Balance the extraordinary with the mundane to give the reader a solid point of contact.

5. Use just one curse at a time. Don't have more than one major improbability per story. If there are a whole lot of odd goings-on, as in Peter Straub's *Ghost Story*, they should all have, finally, a single cause. That one cause accepted, all the rest follows: the other oddities fall into place. But don't turn your story into Abbot and Costello Meet Frankenstein, the Wolfman, Dracula, and the Smog Monster. That just turns into embarrassed giggles, not serious (if temporary) belief.

Don't cross genres, either. Don't have what, for 2/3 of the

story, we're led to believe is a normal (if insane) mass murderer, in a police-procedural sort of story, and then change gears and reveal that the murderer is a filthy Arcturan spy after our electromagnetic secrets or a Neanderthal thawed from a handy nearby glacier. State your rules, make your promises, at the outset; then stick to them.

However, you're free to extrapolate, as Stephen King does in *'Salem's Lot*. His premise is your basic vampire. His extrapolation is that, in an isolated town with only so many bite-ees available, one vampire with one victim per night would lead very shortly, by geometric progression, to virtually everybody in town's becoming vampiric. (One bites one; two bite two, the following night, for a total of four; four bite four more, and now there are eight, just in three days, and so on.) That's a valid, reasonable extrapolation from the initial premise. Science fiction does a lot of similar extrapolations—one speculative hypothesis, and then the rest solidly logical and reasonable, given that initial premise.

Keep to one central premise, and what hangs by it. Refrain from throwing in kitchen sinks.

6. Don't undercut your curse. Don't play it for laughs, ever, if you want it otherwise taken seriously. Don't show it was all a dream, or not really a curse at all, or all due to a fever hitherto unknown to science. A contemporary reader's belief isn't too hard to earn, but can be lost in a flash. Don't explain your curse away or make fun of it. Your monster can show up wearing a Mickey Mouse watch (or, as in the case of King's *It*, a clown suit)—but it'd better be a *very sinister* Mickey Mouse watch, worn for a solid and serious reason, not because you're laughing at your own story and making it look silly. That has all the charm of a comedian getting hysterics over his own gags while the audience prepares to pelt him with week-old kumquats.

Your readers can't express their indignation quite so directly; but they'll flip the page or do something more interesting, like sort coupons. And they won't come back. Ever. Why risk that, for the sake of a few authorial chuckles at your story's (and your readers') expense?

7. Especially at first, don't talk about the curse yourself, in

narrative summary. Show it in action and dialogue, in scenes. As the characters discern what odd thing is going on, the reader will be finding out along with them. And the characters provide a solid anchor (if you don't make them unbelieving fools). The reader will tend to accept what they accept, if you've established them as credible people the reader is willing to identify with.

Dialogue is more believable than summary. We overhear it. We assume the characters believe and mean what they're saying, unless they're visibly foolish or obviously lying. The dialogue is shown (heard), not told about in summary, and therefore has greater immediacy and impact. We may not be inclined to credit what the author claims (until we've seen it for ourselves), but we'll believe the characters if they've been made credible as people to begin with.

8. Don't let the curse either take over, rendering the whole story weird and uninvolving, or become commonplace. If you've got a magical character, don't have him or her casting spells every few pages, or the reader will find it too hard to make contact with the reality the fiction presents. A story where literally anything can happen is a story where nothing makes sense. It has no internal coherence, no rules, no dramatic tension. If anything can happen, it all happens for no particular reason and leads to no particular result. No build. No momentum.

Similarly, an all-powerful character, one who can do anything he or she chooses, kills drama and suspense. That's the trouble the original creators of Superman ran into—nothing was a real challenge, the way Superman's character and powers had been defined. *Voila*: Kryptonite!

If the extraordinary character is somebody other than the protagonist (usually a good choice: remember what I said about bridge characters, back in Chapter 3), keep that character offstage most of the time and center attention on the more credible protagonist. That's why Tolkien kills off Gandalf fairly early in the first book of the trilogy and doesn't resurrect him for several hundred pages. He wanted to focus on the hobbits, who have to make hard choices, not on a wizard who just has to wave a wand and speak some words to get out of trouble. And he shows the limits on Gandalf's power throughout, to bring out the wizard's human qualities and counterbalance the magical ones.

Make the magician or elf (or whatever) very normal and ordinary 99 percent of the time, but with the potential of being extraordinary once in a while. That builds credibility and also suspense, since the reader is always waiting for the specialness to come out.

Michael McDowell has a remarkable multi-volume novel titled *Blackwater*. It's an account of the doings of a fairly ordinary southern family, except that the protagonist turns, every now and again, into something apparently indistinguishable from the Creature from the Black Lagoon. The rest of the time, she's an interesting but by no means remarkable housewife. Sometimes, just once in a while, she transforms and eats people who annoy her. That gives, as you might well imagine, heightened drama to arguments with her in-laws and makes readers take a particular interest in her children's adolescent difficulties.

If you've got a monster, don't trot it out in every chapter or the reader will start to yawn. The monster you imagine, as a reader, is much more frightening than the monster you see. The reality will tend to be a letdown, simply because it's a determinate object and no longer The Unknown.

Waiting to find out builds suspense, drama. Actually finding out should be reserved to a climax, a set-piece. Afterward, if the story continues beyond that first face-to-face revelation, you'll need some new source of drama because the monster won't be quite so scary anymore.

Doyle knew this in *The Hound of the Baskervilles*: he let the reader hear the hound's howling but didn't give more than a glimpse or a hint until the very end. He avoided undercutting his monster, too. The hound isn't supernatural, but it's still quite capable of tearing somebody's throat out. It's not the same threat as was feared, but it's a legitimate threat all the same. Remember what I said about twists, back in Chapter 5? That applies here, too. Your twist (if you use one) must satisfy and improve upon what it substitutes for, not just change it to something else. That's anticlimax, letdown, disappointment.

FAKING OUT THE READER

The other way of winning conditional belief in your curse, especially after the story's initial section, is to keep the reader watching the right hand while the left hand is doing the funny business.

Here are the major techniques:

1. Introduce the melodramatic element by the back door in a scene ostensibly dealing with something else. ("Charlie, I'm getting a divorce. I'm sick of your father's drinking, the way your brother Greg seems to disappear into the wallpaper, and your mother's flute playing." *Disappears into the wallpaper?* Hmmm.) Make the curse seem innocuous at first, until the reader is solidly hooked. Then develop it.

2. Have one or two previews, or false alarms, before the *real* curse shows up. Introduce, just casually, some apparently trivial elements that have a buried, hidden connection to your as-yet unrevealed curse.

Don't have any important plot element or character revelation depend on these false alarms, so the reader's resistance isn't alerted or raised. Don't make them carry any immediate narrative weight. The elements are just there, seemingly incidental, hardly noticed at the time.

In *To Kill a Mockingbird*, as Scout and Jem Finch are trudging through woods toward the schoolhouse for the pageant, another child jumps out and frightens them. On the way home, Scout thinks she hears following footsteps and believes it's the same child trying to startle them again. She calls out, but gets no reply. She and Jem begin to walk faster, still expecting the malicious child. When the backwoodsman who hates their father suddenly attacks them, the emotional groundwork has been laid.

Again, the reader is surprised—nobody expected the man to attack the Finch children (despite an oblique warning from the sheriff)—and not surprised, since Scout was expecting somebody to jump out at her. She just didn't expect an adult with a big, sharp knife.

An effective false alarm leaves the reader both prepared and unprepared—surprised, but believing. Even though the reader didn't realize the false alarm was groundwork, it's been laid and will sustain the strangeness when it comes.

In general, because readers take plot seriously and follow most attentively what at least *seem* to be plot developments rather than incidents, misdirecting their attention (now that you know what they'll be paying special attention to) isn't all that hard.

3. Have a character expecting something even more extraordinary, so that when the real curse comes, it'll seem credible by comparison. In *Wuthering Heights*, the initial narrator, Lockwood, is confronted by several extremely crude and unfriendly people on his first visit to Heathcliff's house. He's shortly attacked by some savage dogs which Heathcliff, entering, drives off. By contrast to what he's met so far, Lockwood takes Heathcliff to be a rare good fellow—a little harsh, but clearly a gentleman. It takes Lockwood a while to realize Heathcliff is the most savage, wild creature in the place. Far from being a gentleman, Heathcliff is an embodiment of amoral and practically demonic energies—hardly even human in the usual sense of the word, much less a social being of any sort. But by that time, the emotional groundwork of surrounding savagery and Lockwood's error has prepared for this extraordinary character.

But be careful, if you use this method, that your actual curse is *really* worse (or better) than what's expected, even though it doesn't seem so at first. Otherwise, it will be a letdown.

4. Alternatively, have a character expecting a smaller and more credible version of the thing you actually intend to spring on him. In Flannery O'Connor's "Good Country People," the homely and highly intelligent protagonist thinks the boyish traveling Bible salesman is out to seduce her, and rather patronizingly decides she's willing to let him. She looks forward to his shock when she tells him she really doesn't believe in anything. Seducers are a common and relatively routine sort of predator she can handle easily enough, she thinks.

It's another matter when she realizes, too late, that what he's really after is her artificial leg. He steals it, expressing his contempt for her supposed superiority and a cynicism and lack of belief far deeper than her own. She's left stranded, in humiliated helplessness, in the barn.

It's a real seduction, and a real psychological rape, though not the sort she expected and felt so confident of handling.

It's a weird and melodramatic story—the clichéd Traveling Salesman and the Farmer's Daughter, for heaven's sake—and yet it works beautifully. The groundwork—preparing to handle a seducer when the man is really something much darker and more cruel—is well and unobtrusively laid. You don't see it coming until it happens. And then you believe it.

COMPENSATIONS FOR COMPENSATIONS

In many ways these four techniques of displacement and misdirection contradict the eight methods of putting your curse right up front and toughing it through with all the compensations possible, which I discussed earlier.

I'd tend to use misdirection in situations of gradual revelation, when a mystery is involved and finding out the exact nature of the curse is the basis of the story (as in *The Hound of the Baskervilles*). I'd also use it when a melodramatic element is so outrageous that it needs considerable preparation, or when I wanted the reader to be expecting one thing when in fact I was planning to pull a switch (a satisfying, valid one, remember).

But, really, these are mix and match techniques—especially if your story is going to be novel-length. You may want to use one of the straightforward techniques early in the novel and some of the double-fakes later on, or the other way around. It depends on what you're trying to do in each particular section of your story.

And just as there are all sorts of melodrama—of events and of characters—these techniques can be used to prepare for and "take the curse off" any strong element in your story, whatever it be.

If the strong element is a very complex prose style, you may want to balance it with vivid, direct happenings and simplified, exaggerated characters, the way Faulkner often does. If it's a lot of unavoidable and concentrated exposition, as often happens in mysteries, science fiction, and fantasy, melodrama may come to your rescue, keeping the story moving until the necessary explanations are done.

Melodrama can be a compensation for any narrative element which tends to distract attention from the story and the characters. It's so strong that it's impossible to ignore, and the story falls back into an effective balance between showing and telling.

But melodrama, in turn, needs compensation because the reality it presents is so exaggerated and intense. Whether you choose techniques of straightforward preparation or buried preparation, you can use melodrama to show a heightened reality even truer than our more mixed and muddled everyday existence, where things seldom show as clearly what they are and what they mean as fiction can, and life is seldom so interesting and exciting as a story.

CHAPTER 8

PATTERNS, MIRRORS, AND ECHOES

I'VE SAID THAT EVERY STORY makes promises to its readers, promises the writer has to take care to keep. Mostly, those promises are unspoken ones. And some are made indirectly, through pattern.

Just by writing, you're choosing what happens and what doesn't, what's possible in your little world and what isn't. What your characters are concerned about becomes, automatically, your story's concern as well. The kinds of people whom you select as your characters—their attitudes and capacities, the kind of relationships they get into—all are going to add up to something.

Detail on detail, incident on incident, character on character, the pattern begins to form: the implicit rules and realities of your fictional world. A reader may not notice the patterns at first, at least not consciously; but if they're carefully orchestrated and controlled, they're what hold your story together, give it both diversity and unity, and make it specially your own.

With enough accumulated detail, a shape starts to form. Any two dots define a line; any three, a triangle. Even yarrow stalks, tea leaves, and random Tarot cards fall into patterns from which people attempt to read meanings. It's part of the way the human mind works: finding faces in clouds, seeking shape, seeking meaning. So how could your story, which certainly has more intrinsic significance than a few soggy tea leaves, hope to escape?

94

Patterns are going to happen. The question is whether you're going to guide them into symmetry and significance, or whether they're going to spring up, sprout branches in eleventeen contrary directions, and then slump like weeds.

The problem, at its simplest, is recognizing your tentative, partial patterns as they accumulate and strengthening them, making them coherent, getting other things out of their way to let them stand straight and tall. The next and harder stage is going beyond basic weeding to cultivating: creating patterns deliberately, to gain for your writing the immense but subtle power of recurrence, the second level of meaning that can only be spoken in echoes.

MANY HAPPY RETURNS

In school, you were probably taught, as I was, to avoid simple verbal repetition—using "however" or "interesting" too often in a single paragraph.

That's not what I'm talking about.

The kinds of repetition that work in fiction, that make buried but not-quite-hidden connections that can hold a story together, aren't a matter of single words. They're part of a writer's larger vocabulary: image, incident, situation, character. Narrative structure. Plot in the largest sense—not just what happens, but precisely *how* the incidents are presented and the patterns they make.

Return with Us to the Thrilling Days of a Galaxy Far, Far Away

I'll ask you now to flip back to Chapter 5, near the end, where I did a bit of commentary on the structure of *The Empire Strikes Back*. Reread that section, then meet me back here.

OK? You're back?

There, I was talking about parallel plots, and how they can be held together with echoing incidents. Now, the focus is on the incidents themselves.

A threat of freezing, in the beginning of that story, mirrors a threat of freezing at the end. A cave in one of the parallel plot lines is mirrored by a cave in the other. A meeting with an old friend or with a terrible adversary, a buried truth finally spoken and acknowledged (Leia: "I love you" and Han: "I know" the counterpart of Darth Vader's disclosure of paternity)—each has its match, its echo. And there are even more connections than I have space to list. And that was a movie for the widest possible audience, aimed primarily at teenagers, for heaven's sake—not a story built with the intricate craft possible in literary fiction, for a readership of discerning adults.

Yet look at the number of connections there, if you stand back from the story a little and take the time to notice them. Look at how thoroughly all the threads are gathered into neat knots, how thoroughly the story belongs to itself.

Lots of fiction uses that kind of internal riveting. If you stop thinking in terms of *things* and start thinking in *categories of things*, you'll see more resemblances, echoes, and outright repetitions in your favorite fiction than you'd ever have suspected. Start thinking categories rather than individual, isolated pieces, and the family resemblances start showing up—an author's characteristic concerns, the larger elements of style that connect diverse fictions as the works of a single guiding consciousness.

That's what you need to start doing with your own fiction. Start noticing the patterns your initial scenes and set-pieces have set up and think of ways to echo and reinforce them in other scenes, later on.

A Case in Point: What's in the Living Room?

To illustrate, rather than cite a finished, set story, I'll use my experience with one of my own short stories, so you can see how the method works.

The protagonist of "A Sense of Family" is a lanky middle-aged woman named Val, a sculptor. The initial scene shows how Val tends to lose track of the hours and the days, absorbed in her current project, a block of marble—a tombstone discarded for commercial use—that she's turning into a bas-relief horse. That first scene is Val alone in her drafty loft wandering vaguely around after a concentrated session of carefully carving and smoothing, as she reconnects by degrees with the realities of time, neighbors, weariness, not having eaten.

In the middle of the floor is the half-carved horse and the intense personal silence around it.

That dark quiet room, of which Val is barely aware except for the horse, seemed to me a good image of what and who Val was. So I repeated the pattern in the story's other two major scenes—one with a cheerful busybody of a neighbor, one with a man she seeks out to collect an almost-forgotten debt. Both men are sculptors too.

A week-old letter Val opens turns out to be a wedding invitation from her stuffy younger brother, who lives across the country. Nudged by her neighbor, Jerry the Welder, Val makes up her mind to reclaim the lapsed family connection and go, but lacks the money for bus fare.

Jerry's whole apartment is filled with a metal and neon construction with lots of sharp edges, reflective surfaces, and flashing lights, which he proudly calls "a social construct"; Val's terrified of it, but braves edging through it to use his phone (naturally, she doesn't have one: she's cut off from people and has just begun to notice it). Platz, the man she tries to phone and then crosses the dark city to confront, owes her money. In the center of Platz's room a slatternly woman repeats, "It's got nothing to do with me," several times, echoing Platz's refusal to pay what he owes, since Val got nothing in writing, no security, at the time she lent him the money. It was a loan of unconsidered but real trust, as one member of the artist "family" to another, which Platz has no qualms about betraying. He refuses to acknowledge either the responsibility of repaying the debt or the implied relationship that prompted Val to give him the money in the first place.

The first image (Jerry's "social construct") is one of involvement; the second (Platz's wife or lover) is a refusal to be involved. Val's reaction to each helps to show who she is.

The pattern was that each of the major people was characterized through what was in the middle of the room, mirroring situations that brought out what I felt to be the central truth of the people in this story's context.

The story's end returns Val to her loft with a bad cold, fussed over and nagged by assorted hippie neighbors who do, after all, supply something like a sense of family.

I think this basic method will work for you too. Look at your initial scene and what's important in it. Try to identify what the basic emotional dynamic is and how it's shown: what objects, what ideas, what words. Then repeat the pattern through the rest of the story—once, or more than once—to show what the meaningful differences are, scene by scene.

Alternatively, think of ways to contrast the initial scene and situation in what follows. Setting up pairs of opposites, or the continuum that connects such a pair, is also a kind of connecting, even when it's not repeating the identical pattern. The road to Rome is still the road to Rome, whether you're headed toward the city or away. The emotional connections continue.

That's the first thing to realize. Although the individual situations in your story may be different, even vastly different, from one part to another, if the emotional resonances of the scenes are at all similar or contrast on the same continuum, there's a way to build in even stronger mirrors and echoes so the reader will see the scenes as linked.

Heightening what's there—that's the beginning.

MIRRORING SINGLE SCENES

Once you've got two situations tagged for connection, how do you go about building in recurrences?

You do it by continuing some specific element(s) of the first situation in the second. Going from simplest to most complex, you can:

1. Keep the second situation almost identical to the first, except (perhaps) for one crucial element. The characters involved, the place where it happens, the props mentioned, the nature of the confrontation itself, can all continue. Simply because the sto-

ry will have developed since the first incident happened, the second one won't be seen as a simple (boring) repetition of the first unless it goes on too long—it will be in a new and richer context; the reader will know the characters better and know more clearly what's at stake. It will deepen emphasis, like saying "No. *NO!*" The second time, your hearer knows you really mean it.

2. Repeat one or more lines of dialogue in the same or similar form.

3. Repeat a brief description of emotion or action ("He looked his father square in the eyes"; "He felt the old, bitter taste of anger and frustration") in the exact same words you used before.

4. Make sure the *subject* or the *terms* of the second situation are the same as the first. For instance, two disputes about money, or coming home when he pleases, or doing his homework; or the situation arising unexpectedly, when the protagonist didn't anticipate trouble, and reacting with anger: the *way* the situation develops being the same.

5. Have the two situations go through the same stages.

6. However they arise, have the two situations *come out* the same way.

7. Use similar imagery to connect the two scenes. For instance, in our hypothetical argument, the person the protagonist is arguing with could be described with animal-like words (growled, pawed at the air, whinnied, bellowed, etc.) in both scenes. Or you could focus on a feeling of constriction (mentioning walls, or that the protagonist is finding it hard to breathe, is pulling at his collar, is getting red in the face, is gasping, feeling weighed down, etc.) Whatever imagery is used in the first scene is repeated in the second. By imagery, I mean the implied comparison between the present situation and something else, in terms of the wording you choose. (Saying somebody "burst into a rage" suggests explosion; saying they "smoldered with anger" suggests fire. The two are *not the same thing.* The precise words matter, and have distinct, separate meanings. Getting conscious control of imagery is one of the very hardest and most delightful chores a writer tackles: it requires you to make friends with words and use them with a diamond-cutter's precision.)

8. Have the overall dynamic and polarities of the two scenes be the same—the same emotional content, the same basic opposing forces. For instance, rebellion against authority; a plea for understanding and love refused; an attempt to be rational defeated by strong emotion. The opposing forces in the scene, *rather than the individuals involved*, are continued from the earlier scene to the later one.

You can mix and match any of these techniques, depending on how strong and plain you want the connections to be. (In "A Sense of Family," I mostly used methods 4, 6, 7, and 8. Each scene involves Val deciding to make contact and being defeated, and both attempt and defeat are represented by whatever is displayed in the middle of the room.) And there's no need to limit the number of mirrored scenes to just two: three is a good number, as I'll explain in a minute.

As you move up the list, away from direct repetition of words and toward repetition of patterns or ideas, the connections will be less noticeable—but they'll still be there, and the reader will be affected by them, even if the recurrences aren't consciously noticed. As I said before, we like repetitions, coherent shape. The reader will feel the story's unity, even if he can't, at first, point to what made him feel that way.

But, you may be saying, if I *do* repeat some elements of one situation in another, isn't a reader going to notice and be bored? And I assure you, not unless you go about it in the most heavy-handed way possible and repeat the earlier scene virtually word for word and at length. On first reading, readers are absorbed in details and emotion, plot and character. Though pattern has its effect, it's just about invisible to a reader, at least the first time through.

Think back to something you read in which, after repeated readings, you can now see narrative patterns the author set up. And honestly think back to that first reading. How many of those patterns were you aware of? Any? One? But weren't the patterns, the *kind* of events that happened, truly one of the reasons you cared enough about the story to read it a second and maybe a third time?

You already knew the plot, so you certainly couldn't have been rereading the story to find out what happened. You knew the characters, so it wasn't discovering them, though you may have liked visiting with them again for a while. No, I strongly suspect that when we reread any fiction out of liking, rather than on assignment, it's because of the *kind* of thing it is, the shape it makes in our minds, the growing discovery of how it belongs to itself and is one connected thing. It's the patterns that the incidents and the people make, not the incidents and the people themselves, that give stories richness the second and twentieth time around.

Patterns may seem abstract at first, compared to crises and characters, but it's the patterns that last.

The Experiment, the Variable, and the Rule of Three

In item #1, above, I suggested you could repeat virtually the whole situation with just one significant change. I'll explain a little more what that involves.

In a scientific experiment, a researcher will generally have two groups: the test group, and the control. Both groups are as identical as it's possible to make them, and they're treated exactly the same, except for one item—the thing that's being investigated, altered with the test group to find out what effect that single change will have. Whatever difference there is in the two groups at the conclusion of the experiment will presumably be caused by the one thing that was different—the variable.

This is the basis of countless folk tales involving three related individuals in similar circumstances. The first one leaves home, is rude to the ugly old witch, and is turned into stone. The second one leaves home, is rude to the ugly old witch, and ditto. But the third one leaves home, shares his baloney sandwich with the old witch, and gets tons of gold and jewels, a magic ring for warding off dragons, and makes a royal marriage.

Recognize the pattern? It's Cinderella and her wretched stepsisters. It's three little pigs, building houses of straw, sticks, and solid wolf-proof bricks. It's the three bears.

Why all this fuss about threes?

One is an incident. Two is a pattern. Three breaks it.

One tells us what the risk is. Two confirms what wrong behavior is. At three, we know the rules, and so can appreciate what the smart third person is doing differently, to break the unsuccessful pattern and win.

If that folk tale was about just one pig who built a house of bricks in the first place, and the wolf couldn't get in no matter how he huffed and puffed, where would the story be? Conflict, but no drama, just stalemate. Success for the pig, but no suspense. Anticlimax. No story.

Three is suspense, pattern, and contrast, all in one nifty little technique as old as storytelling.

It's the scientific technique of the variable, with third time lucky.

If somebody fails twice, in similar circumstances, there's going to be more tension and drama when he tries the third time because we've already seen him fail and know it can happen. We know what doesn't work, we know the situation; now we're focusing on what he's doing differently this time. We're aware of the pattern, the apparent rules, and are concentrating on the one thing that changes.

Instead of two repetitions, you can use the Rule of Three. The first time the bell coincides with the painful electric shock, you're too busy being shocked to notice. The second time, you think uneasily that maybe it wasn't a coincidence. The third time, you've started jumping before the bell is even done ringing.

If you want your reader interested and involved in the scene before it's fully begun to happen, there's nothing like a triple setup to get things rolling. It gives added drama. It directs the reader's attention where you want it directed. And it makes the scene's meaning clear in a way it could not have been in isolation.

Choose and control the variable with care, keep the situations visibly comparable so the reader will be aware of the bell/ shock pairing and be anticipating the outcome, and all three scenes will gain in impact and effectiveness.

Or, in Henny Youngman's memorable phrase, "You had it

before? Well, you got it again."

Patterning for Contrast

Taking the concept of the one variable a little farther, it's possible to set up scenes as contrasts with one another. Repeated elements let the reader know the two situations are similar; but something in the situation has radically changed.

This is the basis of then/now, before/after pairings.

Consider Scrooge, early in *A Christmas Carol*, nagging Bob Cratchit about using excess coal and requiring holiday pay for no work. Watch him show no interest whatsoever in Bob's family or personal problems. Then consider Scrooge, after his experiences with the spirits, anonymously donating a large holiday goose for the Cratchits' Christmas dinner, raising Cratchit's wages, promising to help Bob's struggling family, and commanding Bob to go out and buy a new coal scuttle.

Not only is Scrooge a kinder man: he's kinder *in the very same terms, on the very same subjects, and to the identical person in the identical circumstances* as he was callous and selfish before. The basic situation and terms of the two scenes are repeated, step by step, so that the degree of Scrooge's change of heart is put into the clearest possible focus and contrast.

The same correspondence of scenes is used with Scrooge's initial refusal to contribute to the poor and to go to his estranged nephew's home for Christmas dinner. At the story's end, Scrooge has accepted his nephew's invitation and has made a substantial contribution to the poor. The whole of the initial situation is played out again, point for point, at the story's conclusion.

At the beginning, the succession of Scrooge's confrontations demonstrated the norm, as I discussed earlier; the identical succession, with changed results, demonstrates the new norm at the end.

If you want to set up any strong contrast, whether it's a then/now, a before/after, or something more complex—how a character treats his dog (with perception and compassion) and his child (with indifference)—there's no stronger way to do it than by setting up mirror situations which echo each other's terms and conditions as closely as possible, so the one crucial difference stands out in sharp focus.

MIRRORING CHARACTERS

Two children, one rich, one poor, who look just alike, change places. That's the basis of Twain's *The Prince and the Pauper*. He uses the boys, alike in everything but expectation and upbringing, to show and satirize the conditions of both rich and poor during the reign of Henry VIII.

Two men, alike enough to be brothers, love the same woman. One goes to the guillotine in the other's place, because the other is the woman's husband. Dickens' *A Tale of Two Cities*.

Two men inhabit the same body. One is a monster loving pleasure and cruelty, the other an altruistic physician trying to destroy the evil in the human psyche—Stevenson's *Dr. Jeckyll and Mr. Hyde*.

It's like the experimental variable I just discussed. Two characters who in some meaningful sense are reflections of one another can highlight either the differences or similarities between them. Or, with foreground figures who are almost alike, contrasts in the backgrounds—their societies or circumstances—are demonstrated more clearly.

Sometimes, though, the resemblance isn't one of appearance but something more subtle: attitude, upbringing, or experience.

Scrooge's Mirrors

I mentioned some chapters back that Marley was Scrooge's mirror. By that, I meant not only that Marley was Scrooge's partner; more importantly, he shared the materialistic values which are Scrooge's central characteristic. ("You were always a good man of business, Jacob," says Scrooge in an attempt to placate the ghost, rousing an irate howl from the spectre.) This qualifies, I think, as a legitimate and significant similarity between the two.

Therefore, we can assume Marley's warning is valid: what's happened to him, dying unrepentant in his businesslike, uncharitable attitudes, will also happen to Scrooge if he dies without a change of heart. Marley is, in some meaningful sense, what Scrooge represents seen from a different angle, in slightly different circumstances, inasmuch as Marley is now dead and Scrooge isn't—yet.

Accepting the resemblances, we accept the implications. The visible (if ghostly) chain Marley bears does, indeed, correspond with the even heavier, longer chain Scrooge has forged for himself, even though neither we nor Scrooge can see it. What Marley is, Scrooge may become—*will* become, if things continue unchanged.

Finally, their attitude (their chief point of similarity) sets them apart from the story's other major characters, who are typically models of good-heartedness, cheer, and selfless concern for others. Scrooge and Marley are more like one another than either is like anybody else in the story.

Those are my rule-of-thumb criteria for an effective mirror character. There must be one or more points of plain connection or resemblance; what happens to one must have an effect on or implication for the other; and their similarity must be a unique one, not shared by other characters in the story.

That's why I call Marley Scrooge's mirror.

But there are other mirrors than Marley. Scrooge, we are shown, had a deprived, loveless childhood and felt set apart from others. His life was stunted; he became an emotional cripple. What was true of Scrooge inwardly is true of Tiny Tim in physical fact. Tim's childhood is deprived by poverty (unlike Scrooge, who apparently was born into middle-class circumstances); Tim's materially poor but emotionally rich. So Tim echoes Scrooge's combination of poverty and wealth, but with reversed meanings. Tim has a crippled leg, and is thus set apart from other children—a different cause from Scrooge's isolation, but a comparable result. Tim's condition is deteriorating, and he is likely to die. Scrooge's emotional isolation is also hardening, he also is likely to die, as the story proceeds to demonstrate.

Those implicit connections are important if Scrooge is to believably identify with Tim and take Tim's life and death to heart as having implications for himself.

The visions of Tim's much-mourned death and of Scrooge's miserable end, his only attendant filching his bed-curtains and even his shroud, unmourned even by his daily associates, constitute the plainest possible case of two scenes deliberately set up to contrast with one another. They show the difference, in this case, that being a lovable and beloved person can make, as compared to being "a good man of business."

Tiny Tim, in his way, is also Scrooge's mirror—a contrasting one.

The whole story is full of echoes, showing many examples of harsh business callousness contrasted with gentle fellow-feeling—situation after situation, with a consistent emotional dynamic which increases in power as the story progresses.

That's what can happen when a writer is really in control of his fiction and its patterns.

Some Applications

But you're not writing about Scrooge or Marley. What can mirror characters do for your fiction?

They can highlight some central thing about a main character you want to bring out, as Scrooge's mirrors focus attention on the conflict between materialistic selfishness, however socially acceptable, and emotional involvement with others, however profitless. Is there some one trait of your protagonist you want to make plain in a way that's showing rather than telling? Then set up a mirror character who shares that trait in even more visible form and let the reader draw his own conclusions.

Is there something about the protagonist's present circumstances that's specially helpful or destructive? Then show somebody more or less comparable, but even *more* able (or more desperate) being helped/destroyed by it. That will underline the threat or hope as it relates to the protagonist. In the very simplest terms, sidekicks get bumped off right and left in detective fiction so that the author can maintain a sense of threat without ever having to *really* kill off his detective. (Doyle killed off Holmes, but only because he was sick of that insufferable know-it-all, and he was sorry afterward and wrote him back to life.)

What you can't afford to do to your protagonist, you can do to the mirror character, showing that it's possible, it's a real threat or hope. Drastic things, irrevocable things, often happen to mirror characters in fiction for just that reason. Like Marley, they can very suddenly become "dead as a doornail" or, like the foolish younger sister in Jane Austen's *Pride and Prejudice*, they can marry most unsuitably to show the protagonist the way to a better, wiser choice.

If you don't want to go into your protagonist's background, or want to keep some other element of the protagonist's life a secret, set up a mirror who's explained in more detail and again let the resemblance carry its own implications.

Things you let readers figure out for themselves are sometimes more powerful than those you spell out in so many words.

MIRRORING PLOTS

We've already discovered several examples of plots which are parallel, in whole or in part. In addition to *The Empire Strikes Back*, I've talked at least a little about Thackeray's *Vanity Fair* (which splits awkwardly in two, between the Amelia Sedley plot and the Becky Sharp plot) and *Wuthering Heights*, with its parallel love stories involving Catherine and Cathy, the wild older generation and the tamer, younger one.

Developing two independent main plot lines takes quite a lot of narrative space; it's mostly done in long—and I do mean *long*—fiction. Family sagas provide more than a few instances. For instance, Steinbeck's massive *East of Eden* involves two stories of conflict between sets of brothers over a single, wicked woman. In the first, one brother eventually marries the woman and fathers the two sons who are the protagonists of the book's second half, with the wicked mother as a pivotal figure if no longer the romantic interest. This book was arguably improved for the movie version by cutting the entire first half.

A contrasting and generally more successful technique is shown by Stephen King's *It*. Like *East of Eden*, it has a double plot line, one past, one present, basically concerning the same characters and the same situation. In one plot, the protagonists are children; in the other they've become adults. The stories are intercut—the narrative line switches back and forth between them, rather than handling them in sequence, one after the other. That helps maintain the whole novel's unity. Both stories rise to generally similar climaxes near the book's end.

So it's not just space that's required: quite a lot of narrative muscle and control is needed, too, to bring off so complex a plot structure successfully without the book's breaking in half. Double stories that run concurrently or through alternating flashback narration tend to be easier to handle than those that run in sequence, one after the other with no intercutting. It's easier to build in connections and convergences among people and events existing in the same fictional time—both present at any given section of the story, even though in alternation—than when one set is dead and gone and over before the other set takes up.

The plots must be very carefully balanced to keep one from taking over and making the other seem weak and boring by comparison. Pacing has to be very carefully handled so one plot doesn't get lost while you're dealing with the other. Connections between the two plots have to be riveted in brass, using every kind of echo and mirror I've described in this chapter, and likely others nobody has even thought of yet, to keep the two plot lines from splitting the story completely apart.

If you intend to embark on a double, fully-mirroring plot line, remember these techniques of compensating—they may help.

Watch *The Empire Strikes Back* a few more times. Read *Wuthering Heights* or *The Lord of the Rings*. (Speak about parallel plot structures! It's got at least three, maybe four!) See how ambitious and able authors have kept strong, complex stories together with carefully chosen and positioned repetitions of scenes, people, and even whole plots.

BEYOND FORMULA AND INTO LITERATURE

There's another advantage of looking hard into your story's heart and bones to create mirrors and echoes based on what's gone before. It can help you use but transcend formula, if you're working in one of the genres with a fairly rigid and restrictive set of rules about how stories can acceptably be shaped. Detective/ mystery fiction is one; gothic and romance fiction are others. Gothic, for instance, absolutely requires a female protagonist menaced/wooed by a dominating male. Yet within this restriction, wonderful and individual fiction has been written. The same is true of the other formulaic genres.

Finally, formulas are only as limiting as you let them be. There are few formats as rigid as sonnet form, but great diversity is possible within it.

You don't (and shouldn't) violate or ignore the formulas— not if you intend your work to be published. Instead, fulfill and go beyond them, making your stories uniquely themselves.

One way to seek and create that specialness is to look to your story itself, stage by stage, for its shape, its proper development. Use it as your crystal ball, to see the shapes of what's to come. Make your story grow from what it, in part, already is. Then no matter what restrictions you're working within, your story can't possibly turn out to be like a hundred others.

Look in. Also look out—to the world of literature, myth, and legend. Many stories are structured as quest/adventures. That too is a kind of formula, even if it's one you choose. Other stories hark back to the classics—*West Side Story* to *Romeo and Juliet*, for instance—and embody their essential truths in new flesh, new events. Other stories draw on myth and religion—the Greek story of Pygmalion is the foundation of *My Fair Lady*; *Paradise Lost* and *East of Eden* draw on Biblical sources. John Cheever's "Metamorphoses" translates legends from Ovid into Westchester settings. The travels of Odysseus are one foundation of Joyce's *Ulysses*, with specific events and characters reappearing in fresh guises. But I don't believe I've ever heard *Ulysses* referred to as "formula fiction."

Sometimes what's mirrored in your story won't only be what's in it: you may, like Joyce, choose some external source as the formula to honor in the way your fiction is constructed. For instance, I patterned a science fiction novel concerning a husband's attempts to revive a dead wife on the myth of Orpheus' attempt to rescue Eurydice from the underworld, which seemed to me a natural connection that might give my imagined world greater power, significance, and emotional depth. If readers notice the implicit connections, fine; if they don't, still fine: the "Orpheus formula" had already done its job in guiding and helping me in making tough narrative choices as the book was written. Such a formula isn't a code to be broken but a set of guidelines, a shape to reflect in a new mirror.

Formula, choosing or accepting some external guidelines for the shape or content of fiction, has been the basis of everything from the worst hokey imitative junk to the finest and most subtle literature. It's all a matter of technique, insight, and craft. The formulas are all there for you to breathe fresh life into, if you choose.

Learn to recognize your hidden, implicit fictional promises and do your best to keep them. Look hard and long into your mirrors, and fulfill and reinforce the recurrences you see there. Because in them, you can begin discovering the power beyond plot: pattern.

CHAPTER 9

PACING, TRANSITIONS, FLASHES, AND FRAMES

THE FARTHER YOU GO IN YOUR STORY, the more things each individual scene will be doing. It will be looking forward and back. It will be taking account of the consequences of previous crises and building toward other crises, both near and distant. It will be further developing your characters, showing them in new contexts, new situations.

But a string of scenes, however good, isn't a story. The story as a whole, to be effective, has to develop a rhythm. That's pacing.

TRANSITIONS

Rhythm is composed of many things: the interweaving of plot and subplot, the build to set-pieces, the introduction of new elements and surprises and the knotting off of old plot-threads, the amount and placement of exposition, the unifying effect of narrative mirrors and of a strong, distinctive theme, and the nature of the plot itself—complex and intricate, or direct and uncomplicated. It depends on the amount and degree of melodrama, the number and relative complexity of characters, and the balance between scene and summary. Some of these things speed a story up, and some slow it down. A story needs both speed and deliberate build, fireworks and thoughtful times.

To unite all these disparate elements, these different speeds, into one coherent story, you need strong, judicious, and effective transitions.

Scenes that run directly into other scenes can be like beads on a string, isolated and bumpy to follow. Sometimes a span of time needs bridging or a change of viewpoint or setting needs preparing for. Sometimes you need to give an overview to compensate for a series of close-focus events, to show an overall meaning or development.

That's the job of transitions.

They come in all sizes. Transition can be a carefully chosen sentence at the end of a scene and another at the beginning of the next. It can be a lead-in paragraph to a new section. It can be several pages of narrative summary, or even a scene that will develop things your story is going to need soon. A stretch of exposition can also serve transitional purposes.

Something Continues

When you've completed one scene and are ready to begin the next, especially when there's likely to be a rough shift, a jagged change, choose something to continue. Following a single viewpoint provides some connections, but that's usually not enough all by itself. Your chosen element can be a connected action, begun or planned in the previous scene and carried on in the subsequent one. It can be keeping to the same setting, though perhaps exploring/establishing a new part of it. It can be a simple verbal repetition or echo, like having "going" in the final sentence of the last scene and "coming" in the first sentence of the next. It can even be a more diffuse connection like mood, or some facet of the background environment such as rain or wind.

Whatever it is, choose something to continue beyond the gross details of the plot and the continuity of character. These, alone and not reinforced by narrative craft, aren't enough to hold the pieces of your story together.

Balancing Scene and Summary

Anything other than a scene is telling rather than showing, and slows things down. Sometimes, you may want to slow things down; or you may have exposition or description which previous scenes require or without which following events will be bare and sketchy.

If you've had a series of brief and emotionally intense scenes, it's probably time for summary—at least a paragraph or two, or a page or two in long fiction. This overview can come from the story's narrator or, if you're not holding to one strictly limited viewpoint, from you as impersonal, objective author. It may cover the events of a day or two, a week, to bridge the distance from here to there without laboriously following every step in between. It may account briefly for the doings of several different characters, doings that, while important, don't merit full-blown scenes. It may describe present but distant events that have a bearing on the immediate situation.

All such narration stays close to the story, but looks from a broader perspective and a greater distance from the characters' minute-to-minute affairs. It helps readers not only follow what's happening, but understand it, too.

FLASHBACKS AND FRAMES

If you tell of bygone events in narrative summary, it's exposition. If you dramatize them as a scene, it's a flashback.

Flashbacks can be as brief as a single line of past dialogue or as extensive as a whole independent plot.

The virtue of flashbacks is that, unlike exposition, they're showing, not telling. They have action, drama, immediate events. But they're not as strong or vivid as present-time scenes, simply because they're past. I mentioned in Chapter 7 that we tend to take the past less seriously than the present because, for good or ill, it's over. We're only hearing about it rather than seeing it happen—*even though it's presented as a scene*. It's history, even if dramatized history.

Real matters. *Now* matters. And what's real, and now, is what we *perceive* as being real and now.

There's a tricky corollary to this insight. Nearly all the stories ever written happen in the past. That is, the story's present timeline is the reader's past. Anything that wasn't set, written, and published in this present year is, to a greater or lesser degree, historical fiction of this kind.

Some stories don't age well. References get dated, styles and expectations change, society has different concerns from one decade to another. Stories about our own pasts, times we've lived through, paradoxically seem more dated than those that occurred during our parents' generation, or even longer ago.

So why aren't all these stories seen as flashbacks, as things with marginal relevance to our current interests and concerns?

Some of them are. The adjustments needed to read, say, Shakespeare or Chaucer with comprehension and enjoyment can be radical. And without a lot of footnotes, much of the fine detail and topical references still get lost. And there were hundreds of other writers in Shakespeare's time, or Chaucer's, or Dickens', whose work is virtually unknown now, except by scholars who aren't reading primarily for enjoyment.

But there's also fiction that's lasted, that we can still imagine ourselves into despite sometimes radical differences of time and culture. And those stories are set in something I'll call the *absolute past*. They're complete, reflecting one small slice of everything there is or might be, requiring little or nothing beyond themselves to make sense. Each is a self-contained and independent fictional world.

That fictional world, existing in the absolute past, has its own timeline, its own stated present. While we read, that present is ours. Nothing is over until the final fat lady sings, no matter how many hundreds or thousands of years ago or ahead the events (even imagined events) are supposed to occur.

It's part of the willing suspension of disbelief I talked about earlier, part of the *Once Upon a Time* syndrome. It's a fictional convention we're so used to that, as readers, we scarcely notice it.

And this is just as true of science fiction and fantasy, with only the most tenuous claims to connect with historical reality, as it is of more ostensibly realistic fiction. Each has its own timeline, its own hermetic present which doesn't need to connect to anything outside itself.

Therefore, what's present is whatever the story's central timeline *shows* being the present. Anything that departs from that is a flashback or, more rarely, a flashforward.

Flashbacks

Flashbacks are past, in the story's context. Therefore they disrupt the story's timeline and are, individually and collectively, less effective than "present" action. If there are a lot of them, they can leech the vividness out of the whole story and invalidate the story's present.

If you think your story is going to have just one or two substantial flashback interruptions, it's probably not worth disrupting the timeline to include them. They're not enough to set and maintain a narrative pattern, so they're anomalies, freaks in an otherwise sequential story. Turn the essential information into exposition. Don't dramatize it. Your story's timeline is already no more than a convention between writer and reader—why put a needless and avoidable strain on it?

If your story is going to have several extensive flashbacks, particularly if it's long fiction, then the technique is roughly like leaning off a roof: make sure you're solidly anchored and the footing is reliable, then go ahead and lean.

Make sure the running plot in your story's present is strong, clear, and well established before splitting off to do *anything* else, whether following a subplot, interjecting a chunk of exposition, or embarking on a flashback. Make sure the flashback is vivid and interesting in itself—if it's not, it would be better as exposition. Compensate with as many echoes and mirrors, to connect the flashback plot with the present plot, as seem reasonable and judicious. Use strong but inconspicuous transitions to help the shift along. And remember that a past story is also a story, and needs to develop characters and situations just as any story does, even if it's only a single scene long.

To compensate for the ending being known (remember, it's the story's past), you might state the past resolution right out and then use your flashback to show what led up to it. That's especially appropriate when the story hinges on some major historical event whose outcome is presumably already familiar. In *The Day of the Jackal*, Frederick Forsyth managed to bring off a cliffhanger thriller about a plot to assassinate de Gaulle during the Algerian crisis, although readers presumably already knew that de Gaulle survived to an irascible old age. I suspect the interest was in knowing the attempt was going to fail, yet wanting to find out precisely *how* it failed.

The same problem arises if your narrator is telling the events of his youth from the perspective of greater experience and more years. After all, he survived to tell the story, didn't he? So you can't create suspense about whether or not he's going to survive. But you *can* create suspense about the manner of his survival—did he fail or succeed? Did he pay too great a price for survival? The *style* of his surviving is still open to narrative embellishments.

You can also displace the narrative interest from the known to the unknown, focusing not on who won the Battle of Midway, for instance, but on whether one particular seaman survived and won the Navy nurse of his choice.

Of course, sometimes the problem of known outcome doesn't even arise: in entirely invented worlds; with minor historical events the reader is likely to be unfamiliar with (quick, now: who won the War of Jenkins' Ear? Gotcha!); or in really strange or exotic societies, invented or borrowed. Instead, another problem takes its place. If the situation is already complicated by some major strangeness, like an alien world or an invented future society, it's risky to throw in any more and merely structural complications. If your story's present is apt to be difficult for a reader to follow for whatever reason, you'll probably be better off just staying with the main timeline and avoiding any flashback longer than a paragraph or so, to keep avoidable complications to a minimum.

If your flashbacks are going to run through the whole of a

novel, treat them as what they are: another parallel and relatively equal plot, or as main plot and subplot, one running in the present, the other in the past, as I discussed in the last chapter.

Frames

What if you only want two flashes—one at the beginning, and the other at the end? The narrator, at the age of 40-some, is going to tell the events that happened when she was 20. Then we leave the narrator and jump directly into the story, with no other departures. The story's main timeline is therefore anchored in the 20-year-old events. *That's* the story's present. The 40-year-old who introduces things exists in that curious construction, a flashforward.

An introductory flashforward of this sort is used in du Maurier's *Rebecca* to set this gothic story's mood of brooding uncertainty. Then the timeline drops back a few years and proceeds sequentially until it again reaches the time the story opened with. King's *'Salem's Lot* uses the same technique.

Other stories have no overlap (save perhaps the continuing narrator) between opening flash, story, and closing flash. The flashes are one time; the story is another. In either case, it's the story's main plot that establishes what the timeline is, regardless of any introductory flash.

All these kinds of arrangement constitute what's called a frame. It's used when an author feels some kind of bridge to the story's basic situation is needed—to put things in the proper perspective (as in Conrad's *Lord Jim*), establish a social context to which the main protagonist will be a stranger, provide solid credibility for a story otherwise likely to be taken as fantasy (James' *The Turn of the Screw*), hint at a climax the reader can thereafter look forward to reaching, or do some other important narrative chore the story itself will be too busy to do as economically or strongly.

To get technical for a minute, an opening flash with the "past" story following sequentially thereafter is a flashforward, sometimes called a prologue; an end-flash is an epilogue. A prologue or epilogue stands aside from the story and comments on it from a different perspective.

Matching and connected flashes at beginning and end, mirroring one another—which may or may not be actually labeled as prologue and epilogue—constitute a frame.

Stand-alone prologues are still fairly common; epilogues are less so—in part, I think, because they've been so severely abused in the past. Epilogues in which the author rambles on self-indulgently about everything that happens to the main characters for the rest of their natural lives, or tries (generally unconvincingly) to tie up all the loose threads of an untidy plot, became justly notorious in the past century.

And there's another problem with epilogues: the story is already over. Epilogues which aren't part of a frame presenting an independent miniplot therefore have no drama and are pure talk. Pure exposition. Soggy anticlimax.

If there's no overriding reason to do otherwise, get the story done and then close the curtain as quickly as possible, while the reader is still halfway wanting more, as I'll discuss in more detail in the next chapter.

Don't dither. Avoid weak, throat-clearing closes, just as you'd avoid throat-clearing, inconclusive openings. Let the ending be the ending, without waffling afterthoughts.

But if there's some solid narrative reason (not just trying to do in five pages what you failed to do in 200) to have a stand-alone epilogue, make it a scene rather than exposition and make sure it has a point, some new insight the story would be incomplete without (please: not "It was all a dream"! It's far, far too late, at that point, to change the rules!). Follow the good manners of departure: say goodbye firmly and briskly, then get yourself gone.

The only trick to creating a frame, prologue, or epilogue is to keep it brief, direct, and interesting. The frame isn't the picture. It's just support and context for the picture. Keep it to that, and you shouldn't have any trouble.

In Search of Elegance

All this structural hanky-panky isn't something to engage in just for the fun of it. Any departure from linear, sequential storytelling is going to make the story harder to read and call attention to the container rather than the content, the technique rather than the story those techniques should be serving.

There's a principle called "elegance" which means that a theory or an object has no excess parts. It may be very complex, but it's as simple as it can be and still work. This applies to fiction, too. Don't use a frame or a flashback if the story can be well told by following the King of Hearts' advice: "Begin at the beginning, and go on till you come to the end: then stop."

Keep your transitions strong; be as simple as you can; strive for elegance.

CHAPTER 10

WHEN YOU COME TO THE END, STOP

ENDINGS COME IN TWO BASIC SHAPES—circular and linear— each with potential strengths and dangers. They also come in three major flavors—happy, unhappy, and a mix. Which combination of shape and flavor will be right for your story is the final major structural decision you'll have to make. And your choice will depend on what kind of a story you're trying to tell: one that rises to a point of climax, or one that returns home to tell the tale.

WHEN BEGINNING AND END CONNECT: CIRCULAR STORIES

The end of a story is much more like the beginning than it's like the middle. Middles have ups and downs, characters coming and going, intermediate crises. But a beginning focuses down from vague, cloudy Everything to a particular Something—a single vivid problem, a situation, a central character. The middle broadens out to create a diverse reality. Then the end brings Everything, all the story's varied motions, down to a particular Something again: a single, crucial action.

Because ends are so like beginnings, many writers deliberately invite readers to compare the two, with similar situations, the same characters involved, perhaps even echoes of dialogue or imagery at both ends of their stories. Or beginning and end may contrast in selected, significant ways while still remaining visibly comparable, related, as I discussed in the last chapter. Beginning and end then touch, connect, form a circle.

With circular strategy, the story becomes visibly one thing, united, a trip away and a return rather than a linear journey ending at a foreign destination unguessed at the start.

Now, I'm not talking about frames here, but the story proper. Frames are like bookends, supporting the story from outside and made of a visibly different substance. With circular stories, the main plot curves back to connect, in significant ways, with the beginning.

Quest-adventure stories usually have this shape. The major character sets out to find or learn or do something, passes through trials along the way, and finally succeeds (or at least survives), often at great personal cost. But that's not the end. Having won through, such characters then return home—in part to be rewarded, but in part to share the benefits of their experience with their family, tribe, or nation, whether those benefits be tangible treasure or intangible insight and wisdom.

That's the shape of many fantasies, which are frequently structured as quest-adventures. Alice, having dismissed the characters of Wonderland as "nothing but a pack of cards," wakes to find herself again at home. Dorothy, having learned that "there's no place like home," returns to Kansas and is reconciled with ordinary life. Although the bulk of *The Lord of the Rings* chronicles the hobbits' travels to very exotic places indeed, the trilogy ends in Hobbiton, in the same place and among the same characters with which it began.

If your story shows someone going out to grow or change or achieve and then bring that growth, change, or achievement to alter his or her pre-existing everyday life, then it's a circular story. And it needs a solid and appropriate ending to bring things full circle.

Techniques of Circular Endings

The circular ending is a kind of before/after, then/now contrast. Since beginning and end are comparable but not quite identical, there are clear opportunities for mirroring, for running a kind of experiment with a particular variable, as discussed in Chapter 8. Circular strategy offers possibilities for irony and satire—the disproportion between the way things are and the way they either ought to be or the way we wish they were—because the reader is encouraged to compare the before and the after. The contrast, bitter or sweet, is plain to see.

Establishing the new norm, the way things are going to be from here on, needn't mean coming home in a strictly literal sense. As all of us know who have changed houses, cities, and even states more than once in our lifetimes, "home" is a state of mind. It's where you live, what means "home" to you. Similarly, if the mood, meaning, and emotional dynamic of two places or situations are the same, in some sense they're subjectively the same place, the same situation. They're experienced more or less the same, even if the addresses are different. "Coming home," in a circular story, just means returning to a place, mood, or situation that's related in clear, meaningful ways to counterparts in the story's beginning.

Circular stories tend to end quietly, in repose. If there's a slam-bang action scene, it's not at the story's absolute end—rather it's the scene immediately before the end. It provides the crisis, the change, that makes the new norm possible.

Setting up a clear contrast (before/after, then/now) highlights the variable, the thing that's changed, the story's turning point. That's the pattern in *A Christmas Carol*, highlighting Scrooge's change of heart brought about by his experiences among the spirits. That's also the pattern in Richard Adams' *Watership Down*. After the defeat of the invading army of rabbits, the story doesn't end. It goes past, into peace, into the "new norm" which Hazel's good leadership, Fiver's visions, and Bigwig's bravery have made possible. The ending, showing life in a contented rabbit community where visions are respected and the weak protected, is contrasted implicitly with the opening, which showed a warren where visions were ignored and ridiculed, and the weak were bullied. We see what Hazel and his followers have achieved. The story is circular, even ending at the same season of the year in which it began.

If you want the quiet strength which a circular story can lend, build in mirrors as strongly as you can. Build in circular and recurring things: seasons turning and returning, day opening and dropping into twilight, holidays or other special events that faithfully recur. Show that the beginning and the end belong to one another, and show that without the middle, nothing would have changed—that the middle, up to final crisis, was a turning point.

A circular story is all one motion. If beginning and end aren't strongly tied, the result will be inconclusive, unsatisfactory, a letdown, however interesting in itself. It's *not* by itself: it has the whole weight of the story resting on it, and must reflect the coming to a dynamic stability of all the major forces that produced it, now in repose. It's not just the final scene: it's the culmination of the whole story—beginning and middle—and should reflect that entire progression.

If beginning and end are tied but there's no turning point in the middle, your story will, in retrospect, seem to have been a great deal of fuss about not much of anything—a long journey to get no place in particular. Although Dorothy may start from and return to dull, commonplace Kansas, in between, she's been to Oz. Make sure your story has been somewhere worth the reader's journey too, and that the end isn't just a replay of the beginning but is changed by what's happened in the meantime.

When Circular Endings Go Wrong

The most likely problems—beginning and end poorly connected or lacking a definite turning point—aren't all that can go wrong. Some problems can happen to any kind of story, and I'll get to those in a minute. But there are two other problems to which circular stories are especially prone. Knowing what they are will help you watch out for them.

Lost in exposition

One problem is assuming that, because the story continues beyond the final confrontation, it doesn't have any plot chores to

do. Such an ending can turn into something like a Victorian epilogue, babbling on about what happens to major (or even minor)
characters for the next thirty years or so. There's no development, no plot, nothing but the author droning on until eventually the story falls dead of exhaustion.

Circular endings *do* have a job: showing the homecoming,
the new norm; establishing how the middle (turning point) matters; bringing the story full circle.

After they've done their proper work in as direct and compact a way as possible, they should shut up.

No homecoming

Another problem is stopping the story short at the conclusion of your final confrontation, your Big Scene. Ending with a
bang is fine for a linear story, but it short-circuits the potential
strengths of structure and of resolution which make circular stories special.

After the gunfight and the defeat of the hired killer, Shane
pauses for a moment to reassure the boy who's the story's narrator and then rides off alone, mirroring the story's opening in reverse order. *Shane* ends as it began, with a lone horseman in the
distance, being watched by a young boy; but neither Shane nor
the boy is precisely what he was at the outset. They're no longer
strangers—to each other, or to the reader. The reader knows
how each has changed the other's life for the better. Peace is now
possible—the new norm.

Although we don't expect either man or boy to live blithely
happily ever after, and although the story ends with a parting, a
final farewell, we know both Shane and the boy are going to be
all right now. This story is over, and it's a positive resolution even
though not precisely a "happy" ending. We don't need the details. We know that something of importance has happened and
now is resolved.

The close of *Gone with the Wind* seems even grimmer, if we
consider only the gross facts of the situation. Rhett has finally
left Scarlett for good. Her sole child has died. She has no husband and no way of supporting herself. None of these things is

developed any further. They're left as flat facts, final.

But the story's main issue was Scarlett's resiliency and courage in defending and maintaining Tara, her home, and only secondarily her stormy romance with Rhett. Rhett's walking out is the crisis which leaves Scarlett alone again at the story's center—again the sole mistress of Tara. Whatever she may have lost, she still has that. And when she echoes the line that's helped her survive so many past crises, "I'll think about it tomorrow," we believe that somehow she'll cope and survive, and so will Tara, just as they always have.

That's all the resolution needed to make the ending a complete, satisfying one. The important things are settled—not every possible thing the author might have dragged the story out to explain.

And ending with an implicit reminder to the reader of Scarlett's proven (sometimes ruthless) ability to survive makes this story's close, like that of *Shane*, upbeat and positive in mood. It emphasizes Scarlett's essential identity—the lady of Tara, then, now, and always—and her characteristic refusal to accept defeat, even amid the wreckage of her life. We know she'll get by somehow—dead child, no money, lost lover notwithstanding. And that makes it a happy ending.

If you want the power of circularity and connectedness for your story, bring it back, bring it home first. Then let it be over.

LINEAR ENDINGS

Many stories demonstrate a more linear strategy. The story is a jagged, uphill journey, with building suspense, sudden slides, and occasional diversions in one direction or another, until at last it reaches the summit: the highest point of conflict, the make-or-break confrontation. Companions on the journey have come and gone, and finally it's just the two major opposing forces left and the characters who exemplify them. Once the result is known, the story is over. Anything afterward would be just downhill, anticlimax.

Most genre fiction, particularly mystery, adventure, and

suspense, has this pattern: drive straight toward a single goal and stop when it's been achieved. Ending right after the crisis, which would be a fault in a circular story, becomes a strength and a virtue in a linear one.

The Maltese Falcon centers on Sam Spade's involvement with what we gradually learn is the ongoing search for "the black bird." The story begins with a mysterious client and the soon-following murder of Spade's partner, Miles Archer. Finding the falcon doesn't settle things. Even revealing the falcon to be a fake doesn't settle things. The falcon is a fictional prop, a pretext, not the story's central issue. We know that because when the matter of the falcon has been resolved as far as it can be in this present story—the falcon's a fake, the real falcon has yet to be found—the story still isn't over.

Remember that. What finishes a linear story is going to be seen, by the reader, as its main issue. Be sure that in your story, it *is*. Otherwise the ending will be an anticlimax, something tacked on when the story really was already over.

In the present case, not until the final confrontation between Brigid and Sam in which Brigid, Sam's client, has been thoroughly unmasked as the liar and killer she is (that mystery solved) and the circumstances of Archer's death are revealed (the other mystery solved), is the story over, its central issue, the one that continued all the way from the beginning, satisfactorily tied up.

Clear the Decks for Action

Linear strategy, even more than circular strategy, requires a narrowing down as the end approaches, so the ending can happen cleanly and decisively.

All the narrative clutter possible should go.

Any subplots and side issues should be resolved beforehand, along the way (as is the revelation the present falcon is a fake). If you had a divided plot, either both major plot lines should already have converged into a single narrative line (as in *The Empire Strikes Back*), or the less vivid of the pair should have reached climax and resolution (as with Stephen King's *It*), leaving the other unencumbered and clear to provide the whole story's ending.

All the subordinate characters possible should be shuffled offstage, their work done, as the ending approaches, to leave the major characters alone in the central spotlight.

Settle the important things—not everything

With a linear story, one that ends immediately after crisis, it's absolutely vital to focus only on the story's central issues at the end. There's not going to be any follow-up scene, as in a circular story, to tidy any flapping loose ends. They need to be tied off securely before the final crisis commences. Trying to yank them into knots during crisis will only clutter and confuse your narrative line. Your story should then be looking straight ahead—not back, not around. It should be all forward motion toward crisis and resolution.

The moment the central questions, the focus of the final crisis, are settled—not necessarily explained, but shown to be resolved, so there's no more dramatic tension—that's the moment your story is really over and you should type "THE END."

Just as good openings start *in medias res*, with something already in progress, good linear endings don't wait till every bit of the dust has settled. Show the explosion but don't wait until every bit of debris has thumped into the dirt or until the smoke fully clears. If the brick that rose fifty feet has reached the top of its arc and is coming down, we don't need to *see* it hit the ground to know that it *will*.

The moment the situation is over and things have assumed their final shape, that's the end of the story. Not a paragraph, not a word more.

No faraway places with strange-sounding names

Don't introduce a new or complex setting for your ending if that's going to mean stopping the story for exposition. Linear endings are no place for exposition.

If the place is new but simple—a high ledge, the woods in a

rainstorm, a circus, a supermarket, a rush hour expressway where your characters dodge through the lanes on foot—then it won't need explaining or extensive description. Such a setting can be created by citing just a few effective details; readers can fill in the rest from their own experience. A setting like that, even if it's a new one, can heighten your drama without becoming a distraction.

But if your ending itself is going to be fairly complex no matter how you narrow it down, then keep all other elements as simple as possible in compensation. That includes setting. With a complex ending, you might better keep the characters in a setting already familiar, one that's been thoroughly described earlier in the story.

But that kind of decision can be made retroactive. What's new is what's new to the reader, no matter when you actually created it. If you find that for your ending, you've found/invented a perfectly wonderful place you refuse to do without, a new place that would be confusing or ineffective without description, then pre-wash it to get the new out. Go back in your story and use it as the location for some other scene, with whatever description or explanation is then appropriate. Then you'll be able to re-create it at the end with just a phrase or two, maybe echoing a piece of the original description, maybe mentioning some memorable feature you invented for the purpose, to help the reader's recollection.

No new characters

By the same token, don't introduce any additional characters except cardboard walk-ons (a driver leaning to shout curses as he blurs by; a checkout clerk who hands a character some change and then discreetly disappears from the narrative). Keep to the principals.

Making a scene

Be sure your final scene *is* a scene. Not a discussion, not an interior monologue. Make something happen.

Just as scenes generally provide the most effective openings, they make the most powerful endings. And just as you needed to think of an opening which would demonstrate exactly who these people are and what's at stake, you now need a situation that shows so clearly what the final conflict involves that you won't need to do any explaining or have any character do it either, as your proxy.

As in the story's opening, create/select and use good props. Use things a reader can see going on.

Even if your story is more about attitudes than actions, think of some concrete thing your protagonist can *do*—not just think about, not merely realize or comment on in dialogue—to *show* the reader both the nature of the final conflict and its resolution. Actions still speak loudest. So invent an appropriate action to demonstrate internal realities.

No new plot!

Most important of all, though: don't introduce a new plot. Stay with the main plot.

As you write the ending, it may seem to you to be just another scene, even if a Big Scene, a set-piece. What it's easy to forget is that, from the reader's point of view, the whole story is bearing down on this moment. It has the potential for immense weight and power, just because it's the end.

If you don't keep to your main plot line, to what you've been developing all through the story, you forfeit all that momentum and make the reader feel all that build-up was for nothing. You'll be trying to start a new story in the closing minutes of the old one, and no matter how good the scene is as a scene, the reader is going to feel let down, disappointed.

When you're moving at high speed, it's dangerous to try to take a sudden right-angle turn. You have to realize the velocity your story has built up, by now, and not throw your ending into a devastating skid by trying to turn aside at the last moment. This is as true for circular stories as for linear ones.

Whatever forces you established, at the beginning, as the center of your conflict, whether internal, external, or a blend, they should be the forces in conflict at the end. What's at stake should be essentially the same thing that's been at stake from the beginning, even though it's gained added meaning and dimension in the story's developing context. The characters involved should be the main characters and as few of the subordinate ones as absolutely have to be there too.

Your story has already established a context, the rules, the personalities, the stakes: everything you need to make your ending meaningful. You've got all that accumulated power working for you. Use it, guide it, keep that momentum. There's no stopping now, short of the end.

In all ways, keep the ending as simple and direct as you can.

OFF-CENTER ENDINGS

It doesn't seem fair, but an ineffective ending can invalidate, for a reader, an otherwise fine story. If the ending is bad, the whole story can become a letdown, even though the opening was involving and the middle was entirely satisfying while they were happening.

As readers, we generally don't notice parts of a story as separate things. We consider the apple we're eating as a unit without stopping to analyze the texture and taste of each individual bite. We're enjoyers and appreciators, not judicious, objective critics. We either like the story-apple, or we don't.

The more we liked the first few bites, the opening and the middle, the more disappointed and angry we'll be if the ending falls flat. If the last bite of the apple makes us notice that half a worm remains, we're not going to say to ourselves, "Well, the first three bites were nice." We're going to toss away the apple in disgust and remember the worm.

It probably *isn't* fair. But it's true.

Changing Focus

A writer I know had an enjoyable fantasy dramatizing the education of a girl in the disciplines of wizardry. The story culminated in a magical battle between the girl's mentor (a good wizard) and his enemy (an evil wizard). The girl looked on.

It was a bad ending.

It didn't lack drama, action, or very literal fireworks. The problem was that the protagonist of the story wasn't the protagonist of the ending. The story had changed focus, right at the end. And so it was uninvolving and surprisingly empty, considering all the potentially exciting pyrotechnics going on.

This is something you can avoid fairly easily, if you realize the danger. Though it's necessary to have the main protagonist present during the story's final crisis, that's not enough all by itself. Be sure he or she is at the center of the ending, and that what he or she does *determines* the outcome. Bystanders and onlookers don't count.

When my friend realized this, she crafted a new ending that put the young protagonist right in the middle of the battle. What the girl did, though small, was appropriate to what had gone before and proved crucial: distracting the evil magician so that he lost concentration. His own spells turned on him. And the girl was responsible, breaking the wizardly stalemate and bringing about victory.

With that change of focus and action, it became a good, effective ending.

Dirigible ex machina

Another writer I knew didn't know how to end his story. It involved a self-styled prophet who convinced his followers to sell all their belongings and meet him on a certain hill on the night he promised them the world was going to end. Good build-up. But the writer couldn't decide how to resolve things. So he dropped a dirigible on them, killing the lot.

Dramatic? Yes. Credible? Not even a little.

The author's problem was that he imposed a giant piece of melodramatic improbability on his story without any preparation at all. It ended the story, all right: killed it dead in its tracks.

That kind of weird ending that comes, as it were, out of the blue for no particular reason except that the author wants to settle things, is called a *deus ex machina*. The Greeks, as translated by the Romans, coined the term to describe the practice of cranking gods out over the stage to settle otherwise insoluble tangles of human affairs. The whole idea creaks.

Take your ending from within the story itself. Make sure it grows from the characters and the nature of the conflict as it's been presented up to that point.

Whether it's a dirigible descending or convenient lightning striking the villain dead (as happens at the end of the movie version of *The Bad Seed*), the reader isn't going to buy it for a minute. Of course, as with any bit of real unlikeliness, you can prepare beforehand in some of the ways I suggested in Chapter 7.

Keep any major improbabilities to the opening and the middle: keep them out of the ending, except to the degree that they're a reasonable development of premises you've already established. If you've got a vampire, a beam of sunlight can legitimately wither it into a pile of ugly dust; but not if you've got an otherwise realistic (if unsavory) little girl who's been known to murder another child to steal a school spelling prize.

No lightning. No dirigibles, please.

Trick Endings

Since O. Henry popularized them, trick endings have been a temptation and a danger to all writers but especially to beginners, to whom such gimmicks can be perilously appealing. Some tricks, like dirigible endings, are born of incompetence and the failure of imagination. Others, although unexpected, legitimately arise from within the story itself and are validly startling—on the first reading, anyway. And some tricks are solutions to narrative problems, trapdoors to let a story escape the trap of cliché.

Sometimes, at a story's conclusion, plots can run into a dead end, with no good way out. A trapdoor can't save a dying story any more than a dirigible can: that takes rethinking from the beginning. But it sometimes can make a basically sound story better, acting like a chute to use the story's built-up momentum and deflect the plot line with even greater force and speed in an entirely new and intriguing direction.

Maybe the only possible ending seems too predictable—too much like fifty other stories, or telegraphed so far in advance that the writer gets bored just thinking about it, let alone writing it. For these or other reasons, the writer thinks the ending won't work unless something really startling happens: a real surprise, a trapdoor, a trick.

I've talked before about valid tricks, about substituting something else *of the same general kind, with the same emotional significance,* for what you led the reader to expect. You can do that, if you choose, even in an ending—though I don't advise it. It's generally too risky to be worthwhile, if you don't know precisely what you're doing. If your gimmick doesn't work, your whole story goes down the drain, not just the ending. And endings are such crucial times anyway that tricks become even trickier to bring off than they normally are, when everything isn't riding on their success.

All the same, with great care, trick endings can be made to work. As I discussed in Chapter 7, effective tricks and switches depend on proper preparation beforehand. If, in spite of the risks, you decide to build one into your ending, you can't just spring it, or drop it like a bomb (or a dirigible): you'll need to go back into your story and lay the groundwork—not enough to give your trick away, but enough to make it seem at least plausible when it happens.

Chute-out in outer space

The Empire Strikes Back seems to be leading toward a climactic duel between Luke and Darth Vader—the science fiction version of the noon shoot-out on Main Street. Predictable. Dull. But it would be disappointing if, after all that build-up, protagonist and adversary never meet, or meet but don't fight.

George Lucas decided to build himself a chute from the materials at hand, from the context the story had already established.

Groundwork about Luke's father had been laid from the beginning of the series. The elder Skywalker was evidently an accomplished Jedi warrior; like Luke, he was the student of Obi-Wan Kenobi—indeed, one strongly suspects Luke undertakes the Jedi training to follow in his father's ways. Obi-Wan, whom one takes to be a reliable source, reports that the elder Skywalker was killed by Vader—as Obi-Wan himself later is, before Luke's eyes.

From all these accumulated details, by the time we reach the part of the story where the duel commences, we know Luke's father means a great deal to him. It's the personal, rather than the political, part of his motivation for seeking out the duel: to avenge his father's murder, as well as that of his fatherly and beloved mentor, Obi-Wan.

And these details might have rested there, just like that: perfectly acceptable as background information about Luke, explaining and justifying his hatred for Vader. And then the duel could come, and Luke could win or lose, and we could all yawn and munch our popcorn and admire the special effects in a vague, abstracted fashion until the duel was done.

But rather than just grind out the expected clichéd duel, Lucas saw the possibility for an effective switch. In his original stories, on which the screenplays were based, he laid the groundwork that would bear more than the one obvious interpretation. Lucas decided to go ahead and build on it.

He couldn't avoid the duel altogether: that would be anticlimactic, since Luke's motivations for fighting Vader had been demonstrated so strongly. The duel is played out. All the expected swashes are buckled and the legitimate expectations satisfied. But the duel is less climax than build-up to a startling switch that changes it retroactively in our imaginations—not a worm in the apple, but a hissing fuse. It's not just a change in plot—it's a change in meaning and relationship and therefore more powerful and convincing than mere externals could be. Vader's revelation that he himself is Luke's much-idolized father—not dead, but corrupted and evil—turns the duel, and all Luke's attitudes, right around. The world changes, and that changes everything.

The chute, the trick, wasn't simple reporting of fictional "facts": George Lucas constructed it. Though we see the final product which now seems inevitable, as though it couldn't be other than it is, there was a time when anything in the story could have been changed and we'd never have known the difference.

Darth Vader didn't *have* to be Luke's father. In an interview, Lucas has admitted thinking about whether to go ahead with the revelation or not. No, George Lucas *made* Vader Luke's father. He didn't merely reveal the fact: he invented it, out of the details of plot, characterization, and background the story had already established.

Just as easily, Vader could have turned out to be Han Solo's father. Nothing rules it out—as far as I can tell, Solo was found under a cabbage: no parentage, no home is ever mentioned. But no groundwork had been laid, to give such a revelation resonance and emotional power: to make it *matter*. Can you visualize Vader declaring himself to be Solo's father, and Luke saying blankly, "So?"

Not any chute would have done. Only one that followed the story's essential dynamic, one that immediately and instantly *mattered*, could use the story's momentum and shoot it off in a new direction without slowing.

A switch can be sudden to the reader, but it must be foreseen and carefully planned by its author. And like all effective endings, it must grow out of what the story has become, up to that point.

It must not be an escape from labored plotting, but a fulfillment of careful plotting. It's not a thing to do in desperation, because you can't think of anything else.

If you're in doubt, don't do it. The wrong chute will do nothing but zip your story straight through onto some editor's reject pile.

If you're going to have to go back into your story anyway in order to construct a valid and effective trick ending, look around while you're there. Consider the moods and attitudes and other elements that might be adjusted to lead to a different conclusion than the one you're contemplating with dread and boredom. Maybe you'll find you don't need a trick after all. And maybe that will be for the best.

Happy Endings

A happy ending isn't necessarily one that makes the characters grin a lot and start cracking jokes at one another. It's not even one that promises marriage, true love, or victory to the protagonist.

In a very meaningful sense, a happy ending is one that satisfies, and that kind of happy ending, any story can have—even one that ends up with virtually everybody dead on the floor, like *Hamlet.*

The traits that make an ending satisfying are fittingness (the characters seem to have gotten the ending they earned by their actions during the story, for good or ill) and definiteness (the story's resolution is clear, appropriate, and decisive: it's really over).

But even though this is true, it doesn't address the issue of traditional happy or downbeat endings all writers have to confront and settle in every story they write.

Most genre fiction of all sorts tends to be upbeat, ending on what at least seems a positive note—the murderer identified and caught, the lovers reunited, the kidnaped child rescued—no matter what miseries were suffered in getting there.

In its extreme form, this can be a mindless, saccharine cheeriness that makes us want to go out and kick a small fuzzy kitty into next week.

By contrast, literary fiction tends toward the opposite extreme, as if there were something inherently suspect and superficial about happiness or contentment. If popular fiction sometimes falls off the fence on the right, with resolute, offensive uplift and fake happily-ever-afters, literary fiction is apt to fall off on the left, serving up suffering, squalor, and trashcan angst that's as fully a violation of our sense of life's diverse possibilities.

It's important to realize that formula moroseness and despair can be just as trite and unconvincing as doctrinaire, regulation happiness and cases of the terminal cutes. Gloom isn't intrinsically any more honest, courageous, or intellectually respectable than joy. Either has to be rendered credible in the context of a particular story. Each needs to be earned. And each works the better for a dash of the other, like Yin and Yang, opposing swirls that divide a circle, each containing a spot of its opposite.

Better, in the long run, to be honest than either vapidly "happy" or churlishly scowling and grim. Let the story shape its natural ending no matter where on the spectrum of blessing or bane it may fall.

But, with deliberate craft, it's possible to have things both ways. Unless you're committed to unmitigated cynicism and despair, there's going to be something readers can contrive to interpret as a positive note in your ending. Let them.

If 99 percent of your ending is wretchedness, gloom, and doom, if the whole world has been destroyed except for the two lovers and they're not feeling any too healthy, readers will still nod and say to themselves, "Well, at least they have each other." They'll notice the positive 1 percent if you focus on that and keep the gloom and doom no less black, but off to the side a little, where it can be ignored if a reader is so inclined.

Remember Scarlett O'Hara. Remember that Ishmael survived the meeting with Moby Dick, even though nobody else did.

Even death can be positive, if it's sentimental enough and worth a good cry, and has a healthy chunk of true, unselfish love and sacrifice mixed in. Look at *A Farewell to Arms, Romeo and Juliet,* or *A Tale of Two Cities.* Tears, accepting the sadness and passing beyond it, can be a healing thing too.

Likewise, that a character can win or recover a capacity for joy, in spite of great and convincing suffering, makes that joy stronger and more believable. Such a stance doesn't pretend that the hurts, the cruelties, and the disappointments don't exist. It accepts them, but says that joy is nevertheless still real and valid in the world as well, unquenchable as grass. And that's more powerful than unrelieved niceness and empty bliss that escapes the dark only by keeping its eyes resolutely shut.

If you can refrain from depressing the living daylights out of your readers, they'll probably like your work more. But if, in a given story, you find you really have to choose between happy and satisfying, take satisfying.

It lasts longer.

No Ending

Remember back in Chapter 6, I told you about how some writers hesitate, waffle, and try to dodge set-pieces? The same thing can happen, only worse, with endings.

No-ending stories happen a lot. They've happened to me, and lately. In my drawer I have a few beginnings I haven't been able to grow middles from yet, let alone endings. Some stories stall because they really weren't ever going anywhere to begin with. The fault was in the concept, from the first. It just takes writers a few scenes, or a hundred pages, to realize their story has run out of gas and feel it wheezing to a halt.

The only possible cure is going back and starting over. And I will, one of these days, on some of my tail-less stories. Some, I'll just leave, or cannibalize for parts, realizing that probably they weren't my stories to tell after all.

That's not what I'm talking about now.

It's the stories that seem to end, but really don't. There's no final climax, nothing that seems worth all the build-up or seems as if the whole story has led up to it. There's a little talk, a little action, maybe a little scene. Then all the characters just wander away like kids playing sandlot ball whose mothers have called them home to supper in the middle of an inning. Everything's left unfinished, inconclusive.

Such a story seems one segment of a potentially endless tube of cheese, arbitrarily cut at some point to make an end. There doesn't seem to be any reason it shouldn't be twice as long, or half as long. It just goes on for awhile. Then, for no particular reason, it stops.

Some writers claim to consider such formless finales more artistic. "Let the readers imagine their own ending," I've heard them say loftily. On that rationale, a writer could not bother to write the story at all and let readers imagine the whole thing.

Saying a story should have a definite conclusion doesn't mean it ought to have a moral, or spell out every nuance. Ambiguity, with two or more valid meanings, can work; willful vagueness, with no particular meaning at all, doesn't.

A fiction writer's business is to tell a story. The story can be as complex, interior, and subtle as you choose, or as plain as a pie in the face. No matter what it is, whether the most ambitious and literary of fiction or utter and unredeemed formula schlock, a story that just stops, that doesn't come to a head in conflict and resolution, is a story that's not there yet.

Write the scene. Make it happen.

KNOWING WHEN TO STOP

So. You're done.

Often, after all that intense work, it's hard to let a story be over. You've lived with your characters so long. You know them so well now—better than you do your closest friend, your dearest lover. Even if the story has a happy ending, if it's over, you've still lost them *as your characters*. Their decisions and actions are in the past, fixed, finished, not living and fluid as they were while you were imagining the story into words and scenes. They're not waking you up in the middle of the night with dialogue, or creating fresh new situations in your mind while you're driving to the grocery, the way they used to.

It's as if they'd died. You're going to miss them, even through all the rereading and revising. It will never again be quite the way it was when you were writing the story and imagining it out of nothing.

You're suffering from the most virulent form of fiction fatigue: fictional withdrawal.

It takes various forms, all destructive.

Dithering

Some writers won't let a story be over. They burden the conclusion with meandering afterthoughts, Victorian epilogues, explanations. Some of them have even gotten away with it.

Detective fiction, particularly the older, British kind with butlers, used to be particularly subject to talky, expositional endings after the real issues had been settled. Once the murderer had been named and officially led away, or had decently committed suicide in the drawing room, everybody sat around for maybe a dozen pages while all the loose threads were methodically knotted up and the improbabilities rationalized. Sometimes that required the detective to tell practically the whole story all over from the beginning. And everything drifted into anticlimax. But that was an accepted convention at one time, though it's little used now.

Sequel-Fishing

Another way of refusing to let a story be over is to write an inconclusive, foggy conclusion that doesn't really settle things at all. I just discussed the "no-ending" problem, and that's one form this inconclusiveness may take. In its more extreme forms, it can be a cliff-hanger ending that cries out for a sequel because the present story isn't really done. It just stops.

I've read stories like that, and I expect you have too.

Before I had any idea that there were three volumes to *The Lord of the Rings*, I picked up a copy of the first book, *The Fellowship of the Ring*, at my neighborhood library. I was furious for weeks at the book's conclusion, which left all the major issues unresolved and the characters scattering in every direction but up. I felt cheated. I'd gotten involved with these characters, I'd read all those pages, and *now* look what the author had gone and done to me!

The Lord of the Rings is exceptional (I know now): it's one huge novel arbitrarily packaged as three separate volumes for no better reason than that one standard paperbound book physically *can't* be made big enough (or priced low enough) for the "trilogy" to be what in fact it is, one novel. I was furious, not at the end of a novel, but at a legitimate "part" break. It wasn't the author's fault that it took me about seven years (until I ran into the first of the paperback boxed sets) to get past that part break into the rest of the story.

What Tolkien did to me, by accident, don't do to your readers on purpose.

Don't go fishing for a sequel if you haven't constructed, in your present story, solid and honorable bait.

Stories that spark effective sequels do so *not* because the original story was left hanging, but because there's more than one good story to be told in the world they've created. The possibilities of Sherlock Holmes weren't exhausted by *A Study in Scarlet*; there was more to Oz than Dorothy saw in her original journey to see the Wizard.

If your world and your characters are rich enough, diverse enough, original enough, perhaps you'll be able to make them wholly live for you again in another story, some other time. But not by hanging on to this present story so hard that you strangle it. Let it be done. Let it go.

Revising . . . and Revising . . . and Revising. . . .

A third way of not allowing the story to be finished is by diving immediately into endless, destructive revisions that tear the story up by its roots and hack away at its branches.

New scenes! New climaxes! Wonderful new dialogue muttering inside your head!

As long as you're working on it, you tell yourself, it's not really over. And you really don't have to send it out or risk the trauma of somebody else looking at it and (horrors!) maybe not liking it as much as you do. It's all for the story's own good, you tell yourself, after months or years have passed and you're still revising. After all, it's not done yet.

With any luck at all, it never will be, either. It will sit with all your other mangled fragments and drafts and redrafts on the desk where somehow nothing ever really gets completed.

Partly, it's like what I warned you about in regard to beginnings: rushing into revision. Don't try to rework your story while it's still hot from your handling. Let it cool and set into its own form. Let yourself get a little emotional and intellectual distance from it. Let it be over, and be happy with it: a finished thing, one whole first draft.

But partly this problem has another cause. Some writers, losing the vivid excitements of first-draft writing, mistakenly believe the story has died. Because it's no longer interesting in exactly the same way as when it was growing and changing, they think there's something wrong with it. They start on an endless autopsy or, worse, refuse to look at it anymore and send it out the way it is with no revisions at all, in lieu of a funeral.

There are probably things in it that can be improved, but what's happened is normal and necessary. There's nothing wrong with the story—not wrong *that* way, anyhow.

That it now seems solid, dry, and definite, rather than flowing quicksilver in your fingers, just means it's grown up. It's started to become its own thing, rather than being just an extension of your living imagination that can't be severed and survive. But it's only started. It still needs your help, your care, your craft to become fully itself.

Love the child it was. Love the adolescent it is. Help it become the independent living thing it ought to be, free of you, able to stand on its own and ready to meet its readers.

Revision has its excitements and its pleasures too, though they're different from the pleasures of first-draft writing. They include seeing buried connections you can bring out, strong scenes you can make stronger, ideas or intentions you now see ways to embody in character, scene, and action. There's also the delight of seeing the symmetrical patterns of the story you've made, with all its interconnectedness, which you couldn't discern while originally writing the story because you were holding it too close.

But these very real and legitimate joys of revision have nothing to do with procrastination or refusing to let the story have a final shape and be what it is, even with a few flaws of characterization or narration that, maybe with ten years' more experience, you might be able to improve. The story doesn't have to be perfect. It just has to be the very best story you can write now. That's all you have a right to expect of it, or of yourself.

Once it's cooled, let it sit for a reasonable time. A week or two. Then set about your second draft. After that, maybe try it out on some readers, as long as you ask them specific questions and get specific answers you consider yourself entirely free to ignore completely. ("Did you like it?" is *not* a specific question; "Where did it get confusing or slow?" *is*.)

Third draft next, working with *what's there*, not just yanking things out and jamming things in haphazardly. And when it all fits together the very best you can make it, type up a good clean draft (remember to keep a photocopy) and send it out to the first appropriate market on your list.

If it comes back, don't retreat into anxious tinkering. Make a fresh copy, if the original has coffee-cup rings on it, but send it out to the next market that same day, barring illness or accident. And do the same a dozen times more, if it's needed. Do it like clockwork, as if the story were no more than a bill you're paying.

And then, if it still comes forlornly back, *then* look over the accumulated rejects for any insights they may offer, reread the story, and find out whether you can see it with fresh eyes. *Then* revise once more, if you can see a way to make the story better, stronger, *as the story it is*, not as some other story you might try to wrench it into becoming. It has a right to be itself.

If it's a true story, true to people and their experience, and if it's constructed with at least moderate narrative craft, it will be published, sooner or later, somewhere.

Stories are for sharing. Not for gathering dust in pieces on your desk or hiding in some bulging file. Let this story be done and start thinking about the wonderful next one you can't wait to get started on, bringing to it all the craft and insight you've developed and will develop still further as long as you're writing.

CHAPTER 11

BEYOND PLOT

NOT ALL FICTION IS FOUNDED on the falling dominos of cause and effect. Some stories concern being rather than doing, states rather than processes. Rather Eastern, really.

The writer's problem is to make something essentially static, something that doesn't change, *seem* to move and develop before the reader's eyes. Otherwise the resulting story will be about as absorbing as watching a puddle.

The writer has to select or create some structure that's appropriate to the material and that will act just as plot would, as an organizing principle to which he or she can refer questions of what to put in and what to leave out, what to develop and what to pass over, when to move and when to stand still.

The three strategies this chapter discusses—mosaic, collage, and revelation—can all happily coexist with plot, and with one another. Particularly in long fiction, collage or mosaic may be used as an additional element or variation within an otherwise plotted story, as are the newsreels in John Dos Passos' *U. S. A.* or the extended character sketches in Faulkner's *The Town.* (Then, they should be handled like exposition, which is also static and a potential distraction from the plotline: they should be kept brief and interjected only when the plot's running strongly and will carry the reader through the interpolation.) Revelation, a mystery gradually disclosed, is part of the archetypical Story we've been telling one another since we began to be people.

But in literary or experimental fiction, non-plot techniques are sometimes the main organizing principle of a whole short story. The story may contain a few incidents, but these aren't linked to one another in a cause/effect way. They're not plot. And a short story, being compact, can better sustain lots of technical "special effects" than can a whole novel: imagine watching five hours' worth of *Laugh-In* or MTV, or read about the first thirty pages of *Finnegans Wake*, and you'll see what I'm getting at.

All these techniques manipulate a story's surface, make it move, to compensate for the fact that the essential content doesn't move or change. And coping with a complicated surface can be as difficult, for a reader, as trying to make out what's being reflected in a choppy lake or trying to read by strobe light. Remember that, when you're writing. Balance motion and stillness at least enough so that the reader can figure out what the situation is, who the people are, and why the story will be worth puzzling out.

MOSAIC STRUCTURE

The first strategy depends on selection and recurrence, as discussed in Chapter 8. Things repeat, and that repetition can be seen as a kind of motion. Patterns of images, of symbols, of repeated situations and attitudes, have a cumulative impact. Detail adds to detail, each clarifying the adjacent details, like putting together a puzzle. Not until all the pieces are in place is the whole picture at last revealed.

Each piece is complete and has a shape of its own, but its fascination is in how it relates to all the other pieces, the picture slowly emerging that's not contained in any one piece but is the sum of them all.

This strategy is like that of the Impressionists, who built up pictures out of colored dots. If you don't have any Seurat handy, look at a newspaper photo through a magnifying glass to see the clusters of tiny spots that, at the proper distance, resolve themselves into a face.

Let's call this technique "mosaic structure."

It comes in five major formats: mood piece, character study, slice-of-life, theme and variation, and allegory. All depend on the accumulation and arrangement of carefully selected detail. Although the individual pieces may be static, the energy comes from seeing how they relate and make a whole, and from guessing toward the final picture as each piece is added.

Mood Piece

Poe's "The Fall of the House of Usher" is primarily a mood piece. True, things happen in it—the house does fall down, and Usher's sister does apparently rise from her crypt—but these events aren't related in a linear, literal, cause-effect way. Horrible revelations don't normally affect one's architecture. There's a strong element of surrealism and perhaps even loose allegory (of which, more in a minute) in this story, but the descriptions of people and setting serve less to characterize Roderick Usher, his sister, or the narrator than to create a mood of feverish foreboding which comes to crisis for dreamlike reasons, not literal ones.

A lot of horror fiction—"tales of terror" and of "lurking dread"—and atmospheric gothic fiction are structured more to build and sustain a particular mood than to develop plot. At the other end of the spectrum, inspirational and religious fiction does the same thing in terms of uplift and reassurance that all's well with the world. A mood has to be a strong one, to sustain even a whole short story, with minimal or no help from plot.

Mood pieces tend to be closed and rather claustrophobic worlds in which the major objects become luminous, significant to each of the major characters. There's much opportunity for symbolism. This often takes the form of some object standing, either for the whole spectrum of attitudes being considered, or for one particular element in that spectrum. Roderick Usher's house is more than a house—it's a kind of emanation of his personality, a larger skin his spirit inhabits. When the spirit fails and Roderick dies, the house falls down as one's body collapses at death. It's perfectly reasonable, given what the house has come to represent by the end of the story. An inner fact or process is made literal—the basis of most surrealism.

It's important, in a mood piece, to pick a strong mood and to choose appropriate characters, settings, and objects to represent and reinforce it. Using mirroring characters, each demonstrating some facet of the story's central attitude or situation, is a common technique. Another is making the landscape and physical surroundings appear nearly alive, so that they can seem imbued with menace or hope, haunted for either good or ill, to project the inner state or mood onto the world at large. When you feel gloomy, the whole world looks drab; when you're anxious, the world seems bright-edged, sudden, and threatening, as though it were about to pounce. A phone's ringing can blast like a fire alarm.

This kind of projection, sometimes called "the pathetic fallacy," serves to make a story's mood seem part of reality itself, not just a personal and idiosyncratic quirk of the protagonist. It's no accident that the house of Usher is located on the precarious edge of a menacing and oily-looking tarn.

Moods are fragile things. If you strike one wrong note, the mood will collapse and dump the reader back into hard-headed rationality. Don't let into your story any character, situation, or object that doesn't contribute to and share the chosen mood. In gothic romance, nobody has an itch or visits the orthodontist. In horror fiction, nobody Has a Nice Day. Except for the briefest of comic relief that ends up reinforcing the mood (the orthodontist has fangs; the Nice Day is a sinister mask for Something Else), keep to your mood from first to last.

Character Sketch

A character sketch employs much the same strategy as a mood piece, except that the subject involved isn't a feeling, but all the important facets of a given person in his or her particular context. So the strategy is often to present a series of situations that bring out the character's possibilities and essential attitudes—all the relevant parts of who that person is. Each of these situations may be fragmentary—not a complete scene in the usual sense of the word—because its purpose isn't to develop a plot but to let the character demonstrate his or her basic nature.

That's the overall strategy of Salinger's *Catcher in the Rye*, in which Holden Caulfield shows who he is through a journey that involves successive meetings with adults and finally with his sympathetic sister.

Relationships are confined to those which add further detail to the developing picture of the character. If his dead father is important, then there may be recollections or even flashbacks of that relationship; if her interest in architecture is the guiding force in her life, the story might be structured in terms of her visits to different buildings, showing what a school, a church, a theatre mean to her and therefore precisely who she is in that particular context. If she cares more for architecture than for people, each building might be empty, or filled with strangers the story shows her ignoring or misunderstanding.

Each piece of the story should be either a new facet of the character's being or an effective repetition and development of one already shown.

My story "A Sense of Family" was much more a character sketch, showing the nature and possibilities of its protagonist, than it was a plotted story, since all Val's actions end up short-circuited and frustrated. She never does collect the money she's owed or get to her brother's wedding. If plot were the only interest, the story would probably be a letdown to most readers. But the gradual revelation that what keeps Val from relating to people in more effective personal ways is her very strength, her ability to live on her own terms without compromise but also without anger or love, provides a fuller and more ironic picture than the plot alone could communicate.

Character sketches can be structured from the outside in, developing first the most external and commonplace of the character's doings and relationships, then dealing with ones successively closer to eventually show the one thing at the center. Alternatively, they can be structured broadly, mixing the important with the more trivial so that a pattern can emerge. Or they can be a species of collage built around strong contrasts and perhaps the gradual revelation of unexpected or unusual traits.

Slice-of-Life

Although a single character or a cluster of characters—say, a family—may be at the center of a slice-of-life story, the story's main concern is not to explore their personalities. Rather, it's to use them as ways to demonstrate their social context. They tend to be representative characters, chosen because they demonstrate a given social situation so well rather than primarily because they're so interesting as people.

Steinbeck's *The Grapes of Wrath* is a portrait of the Okies displaced westward by the dust bowl disaster of the thirties. It's the Okies as a group who are important, rather than the Joads in particular. They're significant as a typical family who, through their travels and trials, show what Steinbeck conceived to be the main facets of that social upheaval as a whole.

That they're typical, though, doesn't mean they're not highly individualized. Ma Joad, in particular, is as memorable a character as ever was written. Rather, they're a way of making concrete and immediate the human dimension of economic and social disaster.

Similarly, James T. Farrell's *Studs Lonigan*, Heller's *Catch-22*, Dickens' *Oliver Twist*, and much of the short fiction of Cheever and Roth, are attempts to reveal a certain way of living—a time, a place, a social context—as demonstrated by the experiences of a given set of characters. The characters and the plot elements (if any) are less important for their drama than for their representative qualities, persuading the reader that the small reveals the large and that each character and event has a significance beyond the merely individual.

The danger with slice-of-life stories is that, in the absence of a plot to keep things moving, the small incidents of individual lives intended to demonstrate a larger social reality will just seem trivial and boring. A friend of mine describes slice-of-life, not altogether jokingly, as stories where a woman in carpet slippers goes out to buy a loaf of bread and then comes home again. It's crucial, in such stories, that the events chosen be vivid and interesting in themselves and be arranged and presented in such a way that the reader can't help noticing they mirror a reality larger than the merely personal.

Melodrama can come to your rescue here, as it did for Steinbeck and Dickens. Virtually a whole state uprooted, dust storms, cruelty and hope, strong family relationships put to the ultimate test, violent events of many kinds, prevent *The Grapes of Wrath* from ever seeming mundane, boring, or everyday. Similarly, *Oliver Twist*'s colorful details of life in London's underworld of child exploitation and the vividness of individual characters like Fagin, Bill Sikes, and Nancy compensate for Dickens' exceedingly improbable plot weakened, at most crucial points, by the extensive use of coincidence.

Slice-of-life has a tendency to yawn. Don't let it.

Theme and Variation

Moby Dick is an exploration of humanity's relation to the infinite and the eternal. *Hamlet* has been characterized by Lawrence Olivier as being about indecision. *A Christmas Carol* is about the cost of a selfish alienation from humanity.

In some stories, a single essential concept appears in a variety of forms and is demonstrated in successive situations. While plot can and often does help organize that demonstration, a strong enough theme can sustain a story by itself.

The subject being examined and revealed isn't a character or a setting or a mood. It's a cluster of related ideas.

Faulkner's *The Bear* illustrates the method. This novelette presents a spectrum of attitudes concerning Nature, maturity, and manhood in the context of a boy's experiences when he is taken hunting by assorted adult kinfolk. As is the case with the conch and the Beast in Golding's *Lord of the Flies*, each character is defined by his relationship with the story's main totem, the bear, and the ideas of wildness which the bear gradually, through successive and layered detail, comes to represent. And that spectrum of gradually developed and revealed attitudes—each of them static and unchanging, except the boy's—constitute the story's structure.

As with the other kinds of mosaic, careful selection of scene, character, and detail are crucial. What doesn't fit the theme doesn't belong.

Faulkner's story doesn't include anybody who thinks bear hunting is a waste of time, anybody interested in electronics or gourmet cooking or European politics. The setting is the timeless forest, though civilization and urbanization have begun to have an impact on both place and people. Everything in the story contributes to the central theme and the recurring limited spectrum of attitudes, developed piece by piece as the boy interacts with the various characters. Things that don't relate to that spectrum are deliberately excluded. But the range of characters is so rich, the almost mystical rapport with Nature so intense, that the other things aren't missed. They're not part of this story's presentation of a particular way of seeing the world and humankind's place in it.

If you intend your story to be taken as a credible, albeit heavily edited and arranged, version of everyday reality, it will be important that characters not make obvious speeches spelling out the theme to one another. If everybody in your story is suffering through some phase of divorce, the story's implicit subject will show itself, just by what's included and what's kept out. The larger picture will form, from the individual parts chosen.

To the degree that your story is surrealistic, it's shading into the next category, allegory, and the appropriate caveats discussed there will apply.

Theme stories are difficult to carry off without plot, because the story's essential subject, being abstract, intangible, and often highly intellectual (as well as static), is hard to make immediate and involving for a reader.

Again, melodrama to the rescue.

Vivid, exaggerated happenings can hold the eye and the interest while the meaning penetrates more subtly. And credibility can be maintained using some of the techniques discussed in Chapter 7.

Remember, *Moby Dick* is also an adventure story; *Hamlet* has duels and murders galore, as well as a semitragic love story; *A Christmas Carol* has ghosts, a sudden transformation, and judicious tear-jerking; *The Bear* has the excitements and tensions of the hunt, a first hunt seen through the eyes of a boy. Even without plot, melodrama can compensate and help bring theme to effective life.

But the extremes of melodrama aren't the only answer. There's also the solid middle-ground of human imperfection and everyday experience: drama.

As theme stories shade toward plot, toward a pattern of meaningful cause and effect, a story's essential conflict will often be cast in terms of opposite forces contrasting and colliding. Polarities. Not just simplistic, unmixed Good against absolute Evil, but more subtle shadings of two essential principles each with some claim to validity. One partial Good, as it were, contrasted with another partial Good—individuality and self-fulfillment against responsibility to family or community, for instance, or the conflicting demands, on a parent, of helping two very different children.

The closer such polarities are, the finer the distinction that can be made between what a given story presents as better or worse modes of action or being, and the emotional cost of each. For instance, in the overall field of Charity, can you imagine two conflicting ways of helping people—both well intentioned, but one basically arrogant and humiliating, the other more compassionate but perhaps less effective? Can you imagine two genuine loves—one of which dominates the loved one, the other of which liberates but ends in the lovers' separating?

Some of the most profound stories aren't about absolute right and wrong, the melodramatic extremes, but about forces nearly alike, both credibly strong, valid, and humanly imperfect, distinguished by one crucial difference. Does it begin to sound at all like the control and the experimental group and the one variable, discussed in Chapter 8? Because that's what it is, only on a grander scale.

It's been said that no one knowingly does Wrong: people always think they have a Good reason for what they do. Those who make wrong choices generally aren't monsters, freaks, or devils—they're only people, sharing the flaws we all possess. Thus, battles between blatant Good and obvious Evil often aren't the most persuasive or involving ones—it's the battles between rival Goods that lead to the special insights and the really hard choices that are the basis of drama.

If your theme story is going to be developed at least in part in terms of plot, you may want to identify for yourself the story's essential dynamic, the polarity working itself out through the principal characters, and then strengthen it and eliminate clutter. That will clarify not only the terms of the characters' choices, but the value placed on those choices in your story's special world, among the alternatives you show to be possible and available.

If you do, you may find that you've constructed, not just drama, but literature.

Allegory

Like a theme story, allegory has a subtext, a pattern of meaning beyond what's evident on the surface. Just more so. Allegory involves creating a fairly thoroughgoing pattern of symbolism in which all major events and characters in a story have a meaning beyond themselves and those meanings can be put together to make some sort of overall sense.

In its simplest forms, allegory can be a fable like that of the dog in the manger or the fox and the grapes, in which dog, fox, grapes and manger stand for some reality of human experience—that some people who can't use a thing nevertheless are reluctant to let others enjoy it; that some people rationalize their disappointment at being unable to get something by claiming the thing is no good anyway.

Lord of the Flies is, in large measure, a fable of this sort. Each of the major characters represents one particular facet of human possibility as Golding conceives it. The characters are stranded on an island to limit them to their own resources. They're schoolboys (some are choirboys) to underline that they're as close to innocence as human beings are apt to get. And all are male, I assume, to keep any question of sex from muddling the experiment, since it's not part of what Golding wants to examine.

They're boys. But boys plus. Simon, for example, is a fully realized individual. But he also stands for and demonstrates the mystical and hopeful tendencies in all people. He's the only mystic on the island, just as Piggy is the only intellectual, Jack the only natural hunter, Roger the only sadist, and so on.

Other fables are more complex, and whole groups of characters stand for some concept or idea beyond their role purely as characters. Consider the pigs in Orwell's fable, *Animal Farm*—capitalists and totalitarians. Consider the great lion, Aslan, in C. S. Lewis' Narnia stories.

This kind of structural symbolism lends itself to social satire, political polemics, fantasy, and religious fiction. There are innumerable examples of each. Some are plotted; some derive their energy from the tension between symbol and reality, the character and what the character stands for, the gradual revelation of larger meanings.

Allegory can also be the basis of surreal and absurdist fiction, in which the literal meaning (characters living in trashcans or turning overnight into insects) isn't at all realistic but, through its bizarre unlikeliness, strikingly portrays some equivalent real situation.

Hardly anybody lives in trashcans; but people live in slums, and we speak of "throwaway children," those who are unwanted by society. And isn't living in a trashcan a reasonable equivalent or image for either of those real situations? And which of us, at some time, hasn't felt completely alien within our family, as though we were of some entirely different species—say, an insect? As with Roderick Usher's anthropomorphic house, the surreal elements, if well chosen, can become a metaphor demonstrating a core truth by exaggerating and making literal its essential emotional dynamic.

There are two main dangers with this kind of fiction. One is that the message, the larger meaning, will take over, making the characters seem like lifeless puppets and the story, however organized, a mechanical thing determined by forces imposed from outside—a political stance, a religious or social ideology. The fiction has a blatant ulterior motive. In extreme cases, the events and people of the story, as presented, make no surface sense at all. Only what they stand for is of any significance; and that's not enough to make the story readable or coherent.

The second difficulty is establishing the system of symbols itself. The pattern must make sense, rather than seeming an arbitrary authorial whim (umbrella = ambition; galoshes = passionate love; fish = space travel). The symbols chosen must be appropriate both to what they represent and to one another. The connections should be valid and reasonable in a plain literal sense as well as a metaphorical one, and be consistent through the whole story. A knife can be a symbol; but it also better be able to cut string. And if it represents cutting free, cutting loose, in the story's beginning, it better not be used to prop up a bookcase and then forgotten, later on.

In practice, this makes characterization and plotting doubly hard, since each element of the story carries an added weight of meaning and invites interpretation, as though it were a code to be broken rather than a story to be enjoyed.

Both difficulties, combined with allegory's tendency to become preachy and polemic and its requirement that the reader put in extra work discerning the second level of meaning, have diminished its popularity over the centuries. Strict allegory, in which virtually every word must support a double meaning and fit into a coherent interpretation, has produced few examples since the Middle Ages. But loose allegory, in which only major events and characters must fit the chosen ideological pattern, still appears with fair frequency and is a staple of experimental, literary fiction, and fantasy.

COLLAGE

Collage is closely related to mosaic. But it doesn't tend to yield an overall picture. Its component parts remain parts, individual and isolated.

Imagine a picture that's composed of a few newspaper clippings, a pair of scissors and a plastic doll's head glued to the canvas, some big blurs of red paint, and some mustard-colored corduroy cut into oblong shapes with threads dangling out. That's collage.

The energy comes either from various kinds of violent, extreme contrast—surprising juxtapositions (things not ordinarily related, side by side: for instance, a department store dummy with a hinged door in its torso that reveals a photo of a fetus in a jar), or disjunctions (things normally related which are separated or distorted, like the features of a person in a Picasso painting)—or a great deal of intricate detail within the parts (like a Rube Goldberg drawing of an incredibly and ridiculously complicated machine for getting you up in the morning, including a chicken pecking grain, a rising balloon hitting a nail, a chute down which marbles scamper, a dog trying to catch a cat, and so forth).

Because any collage is a diverse collection of disparate elements, it's hard to characterize the form except in the most general fashion. Each work is unlike all others. The classic example is probably *Don Quixote* by Cervantes, consisting of more-or-less random adventures and confrontations, built on the contrast between the way the Don sees the world and the way his more hardheaded companion Sancho perceives it. Another classic is Sterne's unique *Tristram Shandy*, with its blank pages, marbled pages, disquisitions on the deeper meanings of a falling hat, and so on. Some modern examples would be Heller's *Catch-22*, and much of Vonnegut's fiction, including *Cat's Cradle* and *Slaughterhouse Five*.

There are collage components in Dos Passos' *U. S. A.*, with its "Camera Eye" newsreels and profiles interspersed with the various plots. Another contemporary and very unsettling example is Jerzy Kosinsky's *The Painted Bird*, a succession of awful people and experiences a child encounters while wandering around rural Poland during the Second World War. (Or maybe it's a slice-of-life or a theme story, or maybe a bit of all, combined. Collage is such a catchall that few stories are pure collage. They tend to shade into other forms, if only to gain some semblance of structure.)

The Rube Goldberg school of intricate detail is demonstrated by Peake's *Gormenghast* books, with their bizarre explorations of architecture, weird characters, long, meandering discussions of the habits of owls, and endlessly convoluted plots. Herbert's *Dune* also comes close, with its scraps from future histories, royal journals, sayings of philosophers past, present, and future, and multiple alien cultures, in spite of a strong and melodramatic central plot. Ursula Le Guin's *Always Coming Home*, with its myths and folk song tape, is another science fiction work which is much more a collage than a plotted work.

The diversity and endless invention of this kind of grab-bag fiction can create an impression of great exuberance—that there's a place for shoes, ships, sealing wax, cabbages, kings, and even a kitchen sink or two. And according to the poet Blake, "Exuberance is Beauty."

The tricky things in collage are holding it together within a single frame, giving it even the appearance of unity, and knowing when it ought to be over.

The strengths of collage are the startling quality of its fragmentary images, the sudden jumps and quick cuts, the diversity of the elements it assembles and uses.

Collage may *seem* random, but should never actually *be* so. The connections between and among the flashing scenes and images should come clear if one reads hard enough. But it's definitely not a form for a beginner.

More About Contrast and Juxtaposition

Strong contrasts and startling resemblances are the major structural principle in collage. But they also have more general applications.

Then/now pairings, mirroring events and characters, and the Rule of Three have already been discussed in earlier chapters, in terms of how they can be used in plotted fiction. They can also become the main strategies of works with little or no plot. Such stories depend on the energy of like/unlike pairings, on the same principle that red is redder against a bright green background, or that a cardinal seems especially vivid pecking in the snow.

Often this technique will be combined with revelation, which I'll discuss in a minute, to show that things aren't as they seem—unmasking hypocrisy, shattering illusions people have about themselves or others, or showing perhaps that apparently dissimilar people are more alike either than they'd guessed or would like to admit. A bookish minister working among convicts with serene detachment who discovers in himself a capacity for cruelty or a love of the power he has over his flock, might be the basis of a contrast story.

I discussed earlier the story "Good Country People." The plot, though minimal, is effective—a traveling Bible salesman steals a woman's artificial leg on pretext of seducing her. But the antagonist is what he is all the way through the story—we readers (and the protagonist) just don't know it until the end, because he's a hypocrite. And the protagonist always had an inflated sense of her own cynicism and insight into people; again, she and we don't discover her real naivete until she meets someone far more cynical and shrewd than she is.

In other words, the story is a process of revelation of static things, rather than something actually happening, short of the theft that provides the story's resolution. It's a contrast between false cynicism and the real thing, two attitudes, two states of being—and that's the dynamic of the story far more than its plot is.

Another story, Hawthorne's "Young Goodman Brown," has a similar pattern. Brown has faith in the goodness of his neighbors in colonial New England and the center of that faith is his love for his wife. He meets the devil, who tempts Brown with the claim that commerce with the devil is quite commonplace. The devil asserts that not only have Brown's ancestors been "associates" of his, but all the respectable townspeople, Brown's friends and neighbors, are corrupt as well. He invites (tempts?) Brown to spy on a witches' sabbat, where Brown sees arriving the respectable townspeople in whom he had such faith. He is even given reason to suspect that his wife has participated in the satanic celebration. He runs away in horror and the experience poisons his whole life thereafter: he doesn't trust anybody, including his wife, not to be of the devil's party, believing himself the lone holdout, the one righteous man in his community. The devil didn't convert Brown—or did he?

Contrast—seeming and being. That's what drives this classic story.

REVELATION

Both "Young Goodman Brown" and "Good Country People" demonstrate another technique, that of revelation. It's the basis of much plotted fiction, especially any story containing a mystery—and that includes far more than detective or mystery fiction. When a story's main dynamic is to have the protagonist find out something, or realize something, that's been true for some time, the story's motion is in the finding out, not in the discovered fact itself. Except for the secret, the mystery, the story would be quite static.

An investigation is the basis of Conrad's *Heart of Darkness*, in which a man goes deeper and deeper into the jungle to discover the final evil embodied by the unspeakable Kurtz, and of that novel's modern-day counterpart, the movie *Apocalypse Now*.

Often the framework of this kind of mystery/revelation story will be very simple: a quest or journey which involves meeting people, getting into one situation after another, each demonstrating the story's central theme but otherwise unrelated to the others, each supplying some new information on the story's central mystery.

Much gothic fiction is founded on such a central mystery—*Jane Eyre* has Rochester's insane first wife in the attic all the while Rochester is romancing Jane; the story is Jane's gradual discovery of the unchanging but hidden state of things. Likewise *Rebecca*, whose plot is the disclosure of dead Rebecca's real nature and how her widower, Maxim, actually felt toward her.

Most of the central part of *Lord of the Flies* is the developing answer to the question, "What is the Beast?" Most of the drama of Poe's "The Cask of Amontillado" is the reader's realizing, along with the strikingly unfortunate Fortunato, just why the narrator is carrying that trowel and showing his hated enemy through the family vaults.

Some long fiction has mystery and revelation as a subordinate element, but very often they stand alone as a novel's main motion.

The important thing to realize is that *revelation is seen, by the reader, as motion,* even if nothing has changed but knowledge or insight. Plot elements can develop and reinforce that revelation, and show how it matters to the story's world, giving it added importance and force, but they're not absolutely needed to make it work.

In *The Empire Strikes Back*, the duel is far less important and has far less impact than does Vader's revelation of paternity.

If you choose to use revelation either as a substitute for plot or as a subordinate element within a plotted story, these are the things you should watch out for:

1. The secret must be something worth knowing. It must have a direct impact on the immediate situation. It has to matter, and matter intensely, within the story's context. Were Jane Eyre not a lonely girl in love with Rochester and on the point of marrying him, whether or not he had an insane wife upstairs would make little difference to her—or to the reader. Simon's decision not only to investigate the Beast but *to tell the other boys what he's found out* costs him his life. The revelation matters.

2. The build-up should give the secret a context and demonstrate part of its meaning, as well as providing clues. That Kurtz participated in unnameable savage rituals, if presented as a fact in the book's first few pages, would have virtually no impact. The story's journey develops the differences between savagery and civilized attitudes through the interaction between the civilized narrator/investigator and the increasingly disturbing tribespeople and debased Europeans he encounters. It establishes the "line" so that when we find out Kurtz has crossed over that line, the revelation has meaning.

3. The secret should be a simple thing, recognized the instant it's met, its impact not blunted by somebody explaining. The developing context should be arranged so that all except the fact itself has been made clear before the climactic revelation. Vader says, "Obi-Wan never told you what happened to your father." Luke says, "He told me enough. He told me *you* killed him." Vader says, "No. *I* am your father," and the thing's done, the secret is out. It doesn't need qualifying or explaining to have its full impact. That's because the needed groundwork had been laid.

4. The secret can and should be hinted at, as part of the needed preparation; but it should never be telegraphed or disclosed even as a possibility until the actual moment of unveiling. Don't make it one of two possible alternatives considered from the beginning, and the revelation consists of disclosing which of

the alternatives it is: that falls flat. Instead, as discussed in Chapter 7 in regard to valid tricks, you may want to hint at something different but related, or something considered as bad (or good) that proves to be only a pale reflection of the actuality. Misdirect the reader's attention and assumptions, but come through with something satisfying that's a genuine surprise.

Most stories founded on revelation have a double plot structure. The story moves both forward and back (sometimes, but not often, by means of flashback). The unraveling of the secret, perhaps against opposition, is paralleled by the move backward from the beginning to the source of the mystery itself. So the story begins at the literal middle, the point at which the investigation is set going. Like an archeological expedition unearthing successively more ancient settlements the farther down they dig, the story progresses by going back. Both motions should complement one another, so that the moment of revelation is also the moment of the deepest penetration into the past, the point at which the past's implications on the present become fully known.

If your story is founded on some static reality, some buried truth strong enough to speak for itself and have immediate emotional impact on the story's characters and situations when it's finally revealed, then the techniques of revelation may be all that you need.

STYLE AND SUBSTANCE

To the degree that it's not plot, any experimental structure will call attention to itself and often seem visibly artificial. So it has to be managed carefully or the story, the human content, will become secondary to the style. The story may even disappear altogether, lost in the clever externals of its presentation.

One of the most damning things that can be said about a story is that it's an amazing technical achievement. That's admiration for craft, not enjoyment or appreciation. Whole books have been written whose text omits one or more letters of the alphabet. Undoubtedly that was a difficult achievement, one at least equal to making a scale model of the Empire State Building out of hundreds of thousands of toothpicks.

But is that really what you want to do?

Do you want your readers to marvel at all the work that went into your invention or be impressed with how clever and unusual the technique is, or do you want to share some vision of what it means to be human and alive in the world?

Like quick cuts and computer imaging in movies, non-plot techniques are gadgety. Such gadgets can end up being yawn-making, uninvolving tricks as soon as the novelty wears off, if they're all the story has to offer.

Compare two Disney projects, *Bambi* and the recent *Tron*. Each was an immense technical achievement at the time it was made. *Bambi* is a classic, a perennial children's favorite; *Tron* disappeared to the netherlands of video rental almost as soon as it was released. The difference was in the ability of each movie's content, apart from the gadgetry of cartooning or computer graphics wizardry, to reach and move its audience.

Craft and invention shouldn't, I believe, become ends in themselves. They should serve the story, the human vision conveyed in words. Unless they do that, any story becomes a dry technical exercise, without heart.

As with world-building, manipulating the surfaces of stories is often more fun to do than to watch. Remember that the job of a writer is less to perform than to communicate. Don't get so caught up in technique that the style becomes more important than the substance. Subordinate. And simplify.

Use the simplest possible structure that conveys what you want to convey, presents what you want to present. And, as with other matters of technique like viewpoint shifts or changes of locale, clue the reader in on the method, the structural rules of *your* story, right away in as direct and clear a manner as you can manage. Then follow the pattern you've set, whether that pattern uses plot occasionally or not at all.

Finally, it's not the form but the content which will determine whether your story will reach and move its readers, whether it will be good fiction or just another quirky experiment that disappears without trace.

Style is important. But it's not everything.

Now, quit reading. Go write.

INDEX

Other fine Writer's Digest Books are available from your local bookstore or direct from the publisher. Write to the address below for a **FREE** catalog of all Writer's Digest Books. To order books directly from the publisher, include $3.95 postage and handling for one book, $1.95 for each additional book. Ohio residents add 6% sales tax. Allow 30 days for delivery.

Writer's Digest Books
4700 East Galbraith Road, Cincinnati, Ohio 45236

VISA/MasterCard orders call TOLL-FREE
1-800-289-0963

Prices subject to change without notice.   Stock may be limited on some books.

Write to this address for information on *Writer's Digest* magazine, Writer's Digest Book Club, Writer's Digest School, and Writer's Digest Criticism Service. To receive information on writing competitions, send a SASE to Dept. BOI, Attn: Competition Coordinator, at the above address.   6555

3875038